The Spirit Knows No Handicap

The Spirit Knows No Handicap

Becky Reeve

Bookcraft
Salt Lake City, Utah

Library of Congress Catalog Card Number 80-65245
ISBN 0-88494-397-6

4th Printing, 1981

Lithographed in the United States of America
PUBLISHERS PRESS
Salt Lake City, Utah

To my parents
Rex C. and Phyllis N. Reeve
who have made our home a heaven on earth

Contents

Preface

I heard the prophet Spencer W. Kimball in his closing remarks in the April 1979, general conference say, "Seemingly small efforts in the life of each member could do so much to move the Church forward as never before." These words sank deep into my heart and I wondered, *What could I do?*

I decided to share some of my personal experiences, hoping that others might be strengthened by my testimony that you can trust the Lord, that even in a wheelchair life can be rich and rewarding if you want it to be, because the spirit knows no handicap.

Becky Reeve

Not My Will, But Thine Be Done

It was an especially warm day for November 16, and the cool water from the hose felt refreshing as it trickled off the car and splashed on my bare feet. My companion and I had worked hard to wash every spot of dirt off our white Rambler. I felt a sense of pride as I stood back and looked at our shining wet car. Yes, it was clean and I was sure it would pass inspection tomorrow at zone conference.

I had been transferred to Portales, New Mexico, on September 4, 1962, and during the seventy-three days I had served there, I hadn't seen many other missionaries. I was excited, therefore, to go to Roswell, New Mexico, for zone conference. It would be wonderful to see President and Sister H. A. Christiansen again and to feel the great spirit that comes when missionaries meet together. I was also anxious to talk to President Christiansen and to share with him the joy and success the Lord had blessed us with in Portales.

When I first arrived in Portales, I discovered that the sisters had tracted out the town twice, and it seemed no one wanted to know more about the Church. But one day as we were tracting I said to my companion, "There is a university here. Why aren't we on the campus?"

She looked at me and replied, "We have been warned to stay off the campus." My spirit seemed to leap inside me. If it weren't the devil, who would warn two Mormon missionaries to stay off the campus? And if the devil did not want us on campus, then there must be someone we should reach. "That's where we're going!" I exclaimed.

Our next task was to get permission to go on campus. With the name of a man we were to see (and all the courage we could muster), we headed toward the campus. The Savior made a promise to his missionaries in which he said: "And whoso receiveth you, there will I be also, for I will go before your face. I will be on your right hand and on your left, and my Spirit shall be in your hearts, and mine angels round about you to bear you up." (D&C 84:88.)

Such was the case with us. The God of heaven had gone before us and opened the way by touching the heart of this man so that he was willing to open up the campus to proselyting. Yes, we could tract in the girls' dorms, and if we had any trouble we were to see him. Can you imagine a greater blessing for two missionaries?

Words are inadequate to describe the joy and happiness I had felt those weeks as we worked to open Portales to missionary work. I could hardly sleep at night, and there were not enough hours in the day to get everything done. I loved the hard work. I loved the long hours. I loved being a missionary, and I loved God.

The night before our zone conference, it snowed. Oh, I'm not talking about six or eight inches of snow. Actually it looked more like a heavy frost to me. We had to drive about one hundred miles, and since we were in charge of the music we were anxious to leave in plenty of time to get there before the others arrived, to make sure songbooks were out and everything was ready for the conference. A wave of excitement swept over me as we left the apartment. Everything was working out perfectly. We had awakened early, got dressed, eaten breakfast, and straightened up the apartment before we left, and we still had time to spare.

We knelt together in prayer before we left. I was driving, and my companion was reviewing her discussions. I stopped at a service station, filled the car with gas, and then we headed out across the hundred miles of desert. Before the car picked up speed, I decided to try the brakes and see how slick the road was. As I pressed down the brake pedal the car began to fishtail, and I calmly warned my companion, "We're going to be late this morning because the road is slick." I watched the speedometer drop to under thirty-five miles per hour. Then the car started to slide sideways off the left-hand side of the road. Quickly I glanced in the rearview mirror. There was not another car in sight. I relaxed and thought to myself, *The car will slide off the left-hand side of the road onto the sand and stop, and then we can get back onto the road.* But instead of stopping when it reached the sand, the car started to rock back and forth sideways. I remember thinking, *Well, it feels as if the car is going to plop over on its side. Then we will have to get out and push it back over on its wheels and be on our way again.* We didn't have seat belts but my door was locked, and I had the steering wheel to hang onto. I remember actually leaning a couple of times with the car so that it would hurry and do what it was going to do, then we could get back on our way to zone conference.

The car rolled two and a half times, coming to rest upside down. My door flew open, and I was thrown out of the car about fifty feet, landing hard on the back of my head. When I came to, the first thing I noticed was how hard it was to breathe. My rib muscles felt as if they would not move, and I was forced to breathe with my diaphragm. Here I was in this terrible condition, eight hundred miles away from home, and I couldn't call out for mother or dad to help me, but I knew I could pray. So I closed my eyes and said, "Father, I am in trouble. Please help me."

I had no sooner said this than a voice came into my mind which said, "Your neck is broken. You must not move." I knew I had received divine guidance and I must obey.

I don't remember how long I lay there before I thought about my companion. Where was she? She was about as tall as I was, and I was afraid she might try to put me in the car. Then out of the corner of my eye I saw her. She was running around me in a circle screaming, "Oh, Sister Reeve, don't die on me. I have never had a companion die on me yet!" I asked her to come over and kneel down, and together we prayed. Then I said, "Go to the car and get my coat and cover me so I won't go into shock before help comes. Next, go to the road and flag down a car and send them back to town for help."

While I waited for an ambulance, I remember telling my companion, "When I get to the hospital, be sure to have the branch president come and give me a priesthood blessing." I knew I needed a blessing.

It was not long before people started to gather around me to see if they could help. It seemed that each person tried to put a piece of newspaper under my head to get it off the wet sand. But I had been told that my neck was broken and that I must not move. The direction I had received did not say to turn my head to the left or right, or to put a piece of newspaper under it. I had been told not to move.

As people gathered round to help, I would say, "No, don't move my head. My neck is broken." There was one man kneeling by my left shoulder who kept insisting that he lift up my head and slide a piece of newspaper under it. I could not move one muscle to defend myself; all I could say was, "No, please don't move my head. My neck is broken." It didn't seem to help. He still wanted to lift up my head and put the paper under it. I could feel myself becoming tired and woozy, and I was afraid that if I passed out this man would put the newspaper under my head. All of a sudden an idea came to me, and looking straight up into this man's eyes I asked, "How much do you know about the Mormon Church?"

A strange expression came to his face and he replied, "Anything you want to tell me, sweetheart, you just go right ahead."

I told him to go see my companion who would tell him about the Church. It worked—he left me alone—and after that I don't remember anyone else trying to put newspaper under my head.

The ambulance came. I heard the driver radio in that it looked as if I had a broken back and a dislocated shoulder. "Oh, no," I interrupted, "I have a broken neck. Please treat me that way." Carefully the attendants put me into the ambulance, where I relaxed and went into shock. Later I was told that I gave the first missionary discussion to the ambulance attendant on the way to the hospital. Once a missionary, always a missionary, and it doesn't make much difference where you are. Opportunities to teach the gospel can come when we least expect them.

Dad arrived at my bedside Sunday morning, the doctors' prognosis still ringing in his mind. "She has dislocated the fifth and sixth vertebrae in her neck, which has left her paralyzed from the neck down," the doctors had explained to him. "Her internal organs are also paralyzed, and her temperature is climbing. When the temperature reaches a certain point, she will die." The news was grim, and there seemed to be no hope for me.

Early that same Sunday morning in Salt Lake, dad's counselors in the stake presidency, members of the high council, and the patriarch came fasting to our home to inquire about my condition. My mother, who is full of faith and trust in the Lord, told the brethren of my critical condition and then added: "I don't want you to pray to keep Becky alive if it is not the Lord's will. If the Lord wants her, there is no one I would rather give her to. But if there is some other force trying to take her life before it is time, I would appreciate your faith and prayers in her behalf." Patriarch George M. Williams offered the prayer, asking the Lord that if it was his will that I live, to let my body begin to function.

They had no sooner finished the prayer than the telephone rang. It was dad with the news that my body had begun to function. Standing by my hospital bed, he had seen the fluid start to move through the tubes. Their prayers had been heard, and Heavenly Father had blessed me according to his will. My life had been spared.

2

Life Is Different Than I Thought It Would Be

You can be anything you want to be in your dreams, and when I was very young I would dream of when I would be old enough to go to high school and have great fun. I just knew I would be pretty. It seemed to me that every girl turned pretty between junior high and high school. In fact, my dreams of being beautiful were so real that dad and mother let me hang up movie star pictures in my bedroom. Each star looked beautiful to me. I started by hanging a few pictures around the mirror, but by the time I had finished, there wasn't a bare spot on any of my four walls. When I finally outgrew the pictures and took them down, dad had to repaint my bedroom. But a new paint job was a small price to pay for the many hours I had spent dreaming about what I could do to make myself beautiful. I really needed to be beautiful when I went to high school because I had my heart set on being head cheerleader and a homecoming queen.

Can you imagine how surprised I was in high school to find that I didn't look at all like I had dreamed I would? And as far as being head cheerleader, well, I didn't even make the pep club (and there were about one hundred girls in that club). What about my dreams of being a homecoming queen? About the only dance I attended was the girls' choice dance. What a surprise for me to realize that life was different from what I thought it would be!

I have discovered that life offers to each person many challenges and opportunities and when these challenges come, you do not have to face them alone. There is a power waiting to help you if you have the faith to put your life into the Lord's hands.

Yes, life has been different than I thought it would be. It seems as if life is full of surprises, and they usually come when you least expect them. One of the biggest surprises of my entire life came the fall 1961. I had spent the summer working as a girls' counselor at the Unitah Youth Camp to earn enough money to go back to school that fall. I was excited about going back to BYU for my junior year. I had the usual dreams and hopes of meeting some wonderful, handsome returned missionary and falling hopelessly in love, getting married in the temple and living happily ever after.

I came home from camp a couple of weeks before school started. A cabinet company had installed furniture in the new BYU library, and a group of girls from the ward were going down to help polish the tables. Since I had time on my hands, I wanted to go. Another girl and I were polishing a table when out of the clear blue sky she asked, "Becky, how old are you?"

"Twenty-one," I answered.

Then she said, "How come you're not on a mission?"

A mission—I had never even thought of going on a mission. The rest of the day as I shined the tables I couldn't get that impression out of my mind. A mission! A mission? That night when I came home I talked to dad about a mission. "Well, if you want to go on a mission, we will support you," he told me. I didn't know what to do.

I called the bishop and asked if I could talk to him. That night I sat across from my bishop and told him the feelings of my heart, my desires, and the happenings of the day; then I asked him what he thought I should do. "Well, I would like to think about it. I would like to fast and pray about it," he counseled, "but if I feel the same way Sunday as I do tonight, you can pack your bags."

Talk about a surprise! Talk about a life changing in a split second! As I left his office and walked across the parking lot to get into the car to go home, tears streamed down my face, and I knew, yes, I knew, I was going on a mission.

But what about my hopes and dreams? My only real experiences with lady missionaries was with the sisters who went on missions and didn't get married very soon after they returned home. I didn't want this to happen to me. Even as a little girl my whole desire was to become a wife and mother. And I didn't want to be just a mother, I wanted to be the greatest mother who ever lived. I wanted to have a large, righteous family whom I could teach and train to love and serve the Lord. My desires were righteous and so were my dreams. *What will happen to me now?* I wondered, as my mind went back to my youth.

It seemed like only yesterday that I was five years old, playing house with my younger sister JoAnn. "I speak to be the mother," I always shouted, and then I would collect my dolls. In just a few minutes I would turn the front room into a small community, with a section for the house, one for the store, another for dad's office, and one for the church. We would have great fun as we played together.

Even at that age I was anxious to be a mother and to have a house of my own. I was born with extra love and talent for housekeeping, for tending children, for organizing, and for being able to handle things. I loved to tend a baby, wash a wall, clean a sink, and organize the household so that everything was done on time and in the way it was supposed to be done.

I always felt lucky that I was the oldest girl in a family of seven children. I had many opportunities while growing up to tend children and to help mother. I had turned eight years old just the week before mother brought my new baby sister Venice home from the hospital. Venice was the fifth child. How well I remember that day and the great thrill and the pride I felt when mother asked me to walk over to the basket and carry the baby back to her! I remember sliding one hand under her tiny head and the other hand under her back as I lifted her up. I remember the joy that surged through me as I held this brand new baby. I could hardly wait to have a baby of my own.

Since I wasn't old enough to have a baby of my own, I pretended that my new little sister was my own baby. As Venice got older she became afraid of babysitters, and many times she would cry when one came. So to stop her crying, I would tend her in the other room. I remember the last night we had a babysitter. She brought a sack with some material in it and asked mother if she could use the sewing machine after the children were in bed, explaining that she had to get a dress made. Mother told her it would be fine. The minute Venice saw the babysitter, she started to scream. I grabbed Venice and took her in the other room so she wouldn't see the babysitter. Before long all the other children were in playing with me too. There sat the babysitter in the kitchen sewing, and I was tending the little ones. Dad came home from his meeting and I watched him pay the babysitter. When she had gone, I said, "Why don't you pay me and I'll tend the children?" After that, I did tend the children. I don't remember getting paid each time, but that didn't matter because I loved to tend (especially my own family) and to help mother.

Not long after this incident I started to tend children for the neighbors. Many of my fondest memories are the hours I spent with these children. A dentist and his family moved next door and through the years I tended their children, efficiently and lovingly caring for each child. Their family grew, but I was always able to handle the children. I also used to tend the bishop's family, and how I loved them! I did not have to be their natural mother. I just loved little children and felt as if they were my own.

The most challenging babysitting experience came the year I turned sixteen. I was excited because my sister JoAnn and I were leaving the following morning for a three-day summer camp. I had paid my money, and my clothes were all washed and packed. JoAnn and I were babysitting when the phone rang. It was dad. Aunt Marylene had called, he explained, and she had the opportunity to go with Uncle Evan to Alabama for two weeks with the Air Force Reserves. They needed a babysitter. I was excited that they would ask me. There was no decision to make. Aunt Marylene needed help, and I would go. So the next morning I took my packed bags and headed for Sigurd, Utah, instead of summer camp at the Spruces.

It was really a great experience; I had to use all my talents and abilities to do it. I had the responsibility of seven children: Glenn, nine; Kenneth, eight; Pat, seven; Gerald, five; Jeanne, four; Camile, two; and Scott, eight months. Besides tending the children and keeping house, I would bake bread, pasteurize the milk, and see that the children did their chores, such as practice the piano, hoe the garden, and milk the cows. Farm life was a different experience for me. But I remember the great satisfaction I felt one morning when the bishop dropped in before 10:00 A.M. I had all the children up and dressed. All the beds were made, and the rooms were straightened up. I had cooked breakfast, fed the children, washed and dried the dishes, and cleaned up the kitchen. The house was clean and orderly. The bishop looked surprised, and I was pleased.

Oh, how I longed to have a home and children of my own! It seemed to me that it took forever to get old enough to be married. Now, at last, I felt I was ready and anxious to meet a mate who was worthy to take me to the temple. But this particular day as I walked toward the car, I quietly closed the door to my dream world and came back to reality. There was a lump in my throat and a funny feeling in my heart, for I realized that my hopes and desires would have to wait because I was going on a mission.

As I drove home I thought, *I can trust my priesthood leaders. They speak for the Lord. If the Lord calls me on a mission through his prophet, I will gladly postpone my desires of being a great mother for a time, and I will go out and serve the Lord. I will learn and will become the greatest sister missionary who has ever served. In fact, I will be so great that people will not wonder why I did not get married, and I will have much success and will bring many souls into the Church.* These were the feelings of my heart.

But life is different from what I thought it would be. In one day my life had changed. Instead of being a wife and a mother, I was going out to represent the Lord Jesus Christ as a missionary. Yes, I was going out to be the greatest sister missionary in the world.

3

A Missionary to Match the Message

If you were to ask me, "Would you go into the mission field, knowing you would come home in a wheelchair?" I would honestly reply, "Yes, I would still go." How grateful I am that I did not miss the experience of a mission and that I had the trust in my priesthood leaders and the faith in my Father in Heaven to accept his call! The lessons and experiences I gained in the mission field were so important to me that I would not trade them. To be a missionary and see the great change that comes into a person's life when the Holy Spirit touches him is an experience of unequaled joy. This much I know: There is power in the gospel of Jesus Christ to change lives.

Let me share the missionary spirit with you. The first night Sister Bergan and I checked a referral for the John Smith family, I did not feel there was much hope for their conversion because of their life-style. But as we taught them they listened, and they prayed sincerely. Their life-style changed, and I was blessed to see and feel the miracle of conversion taking place in their lives. Following their priesthood interview, a baptismal date was set.

During the last seventy-two hours before a person is to be baptized there is a struggle with the adversary that is unmerciful and very real. Sister Bergan and I were well aware of this, so we had planned to spend as much time as we could with the Smith family Friday night and Saturday. I was not going to take any chances. I asked Brother Smith if he would fix the brake shoes on the car Saturday. That meant we would spend most of the day with them before their baptism that evening. I felt happy and excited Friday night as we knelt in prayer with the Smith family before going to our apartment. Love filled the room, and it was hard to say goodnight. We all wanted to stay where the Spirit was and to enjoy the bonds of friendship.

I cannot remember driving home that night. It seemed as if I floated up the stairs to the apartment. What great inner joy I felt as I said my prayers, thanking Heavenly Father for all his blessings to me! Tomorrow we would see a whole family baptized.

The sharp ring of the telephone aroused me and, struggling with the covers, I began to realize what the sound was. I hurried across the floor, my heart in my throat, to answer the phone.

"Hello," I must have said, waiting to hear whose voice would answer back.

"Sister Reeve," Sister Smith sobbed, "come quick. Everything has gone wrong, and we are not going to be baptized."

"What!" The bottom seemed to drop out of my world, leaving me numb and cold. I don't remember my reply, and I don't remember dressing. All I recall is the sick feeling of fear all over my body.

As I entered the Smith home, the hair stood up on my arms. I felt a cold, uncomfortable fear, and I wanted to turn and run from the influence of the enemy. His spirit was there. It made me heartsick and left me almost paralyzed with fear. The only thought that came into my head was to pray. The family gathered around, and through the sobs and tears of mother and children we asked Heavenly Father to help them. Some relief came, and we all sat down in the front room. The details of what had happened in the last few hours spilled out between sobs.

It seems that Brother Smith could not sleep around 4:00 A.M., so he turned over in bed and said to his wife, "Dear, this is the happiest day of our lives, and I want to make you a special breakfast to eat in bed." With that he gave her a kiss and got out of bed. The first thing to go wrong happened when he opened the refrigerator door. The middle shelf fell out, spilling such things as a bowl of leftover spaghetti, a bottle of peaches, a dozen eggs, milk, and other supplies stored on that shelf. Brother Smith did not lose his temper, but together with Sister Smith he cleaned up the mess. Next, the dog killed a couple of the neighbor's chickens. This had never happened before. The neighbor called the police and threatened a lawsuit. After this crisis, Brother Smith decided to go to a department store to buy himself a suit to wear to church. He found a flat tire on his car. The car fell off the jack three times before he got the tire changed. The crowning blow came as Brother Smith got into the car to go. Sister Smith had decided to go with him. In the few seconds it had taken her to go out the front door and get into the car, the four-year-old girl pushed the baby boy off the front porch. He fell on the step and hit his head, which resulted in a huge "goose egg" and left him screaming. Brother Smith could stand no more, and he jumped out of the car, took off his belt, and began hitting everyone. Then he grabbed a pack of cigarettes, got back into the car, and sped off.

I wanted to run away from the heartbreak, the wounded feelings, and especially the ugly, dark spirit that hovered around. But for some reason, I could not leave them in such a sad state. About an hour later Brother Smith drove up. He felt terribly ashamed and remorseful for what he had done to his family. "I guess you won't want me to fix your car now?" he muttered. I wanted to say no, but instead I replied, "Yes, we need it fixed."

It took Brother Smith all afternoon to repair our car. He had all kinds of trouble. In fact, the car fell off the jack three times, and once he almost got pinned under the car. At 5:00 P.M. Sister Smith came out and said, "It's time to go and get baptized if you still want to."

"No, I can't get baptized after losing my temper like that," was his reply.

We missed the baptism too, since our car was not finished. I felt horrible inside, almost sick; and I still wanted to run away from the heavy feeling in the house.

It was after 7:00 P.M. and getting dark before Brother Smith finished and came into the house. We were all sitting, quiet and strained, in the front room. He handed me the keys to our car, saying it was fixed, and then he sat down in an old chair. He was covered with black grease. With his eyes glued to the floor he said, "I guess it's too late for me to be baptized. I have to be baptized tonight because I can't go through another week like this last one." A surprised feeling along with a gleam of hope seemed to be filling my body. I could not believe my ears, and a wave of excitement raced through me.

"Yes, yes, you can!" I exclaimed, not knowing just how but confident I would find a way. Once again we all knelt in prayer. As we left, we warned them to lock the dog in the basement, stay in the house, and be careful until we came back. A different excitement filled my heart this time as we hurried to our apartment to make plans.

The first thing I did when we got home was to call the stake center. The janitor answered the phone. He had just emptied the baptismal font and would not fill it again. "If they can't wait until next week," he mumbled, "they shouldn't be baptized." I just did not have time to explain (though I felt like telling him the kind of day we had spent) so I quickly hung up before I said something I would be sorry for. *What do I do now?* I asked myself. My stomach felt as if it were tied in a knot.

"Water, water," I kept repeating, and then an idea came. I took the map of Denver off the shelf and opened it. Then I located Arvada, our area. Sure enough, right in the middle of west Denver was a park and in the park was a blue section which meant water. What a great feeling surged through me as I said, "Sloan's Lake, that's where we will baptize them!" Now, all we needed was to get someone having authority to baptize them. Where would our elders be on Saturday night? It was preparation day. We found eight elders all dressed in suits just ready for a baptism. They were anxious to help and told us to go over to the Smiths' house and get them dressed in white clothes; they would meet us there.

It was 11:00 P.M. when we arrived at the Smiths'. They had given up waiting for us and had gone to bed. All the lights were out. Sister Smith answered the door in her nightgown.

"We are here to baptize you. Get into your white clothes," I said. (We had taken baptismal clothes to their house to try on after the second discussion.) I'll never forget hearing Sister Smith waking up Brother Smith.

"Dear," she said, "wake up. We're going to be baptized."

"What time is it?" he groaned.

"Never mind, the Lord has provided the way. Just get up and get your clothes on," she forcefully said.

"Just where are we going to be baptized at this time of the night?" he questioned. "Sloan's Lake?" he cried, after his wife had answered his question.

What a beautiful place for a baptism! The street lights reflected on the water. I spread blankets out, and we all sat down. We opened with a song and a prayer. Talks on baptism were given by the missionaries, and then in the stillness of the night I watched the Smith family be baptized.

What a calm, peaceful feeling swept over me! The excitement and emotions of the day seemed distant. The thrill of seeing Brother Smith step out of the water dripping wet filled my soul with unspeakable joy and satisfaction and tears streamed down my face. I knew God had heard our prayers. I knew that we could trust him, that after we had done all we could do, he would open a way for the Smith family to be baptized. He did indeed. My love for my Heavenly Father seemed to saturate every cell in my body until I felt warm and happy and filled with gratitude.

Brother and Sister Smith fixed us all an early-morning break-fast of pancakes. Once again we left their home, after having a prayer, and headed for our different apartments. It was late, and we had to pick up our newly baptized Smith family for church in the morning. But that did not matter. Completely drained physically, I lay in my bed overwhelmed at the events of the day. I felt warm and contented as I closed my eyes.

This was just one experience and one family that made me glad I was a missionary. I loved being a missionary. It is exciting and humbling to stand as a witness for the Lord Jesus Christ, to be a small part in the miracle of conversion, and to see the power of the gospel of Jesus Christ.

When I left home as a missionary, I thought I had eighteen months to serve our Father in Heaven. In reality I was only allowed to serve thirteen months. In a split second my life changed. Once again my hopes and dreams and desires of being the greatest sister missionary were crushed. *What does the Lord want me to do now?* I asked myself. Only time would tell.

4

Let Go of the Bush

I have often thought of the story of the young boy who was walking along the edge of a steep cliff when he slipped and fell over the edge. As he fell he was able to grab onto a small bush. It was a long way down, and as his hands started to slip, he cried out, "Father, help me!"

In answer to his plea a voice said, "Let go of the bush."

Imagine the faith it would take for this small boy to let go of the bush. I have found that this life requires great faith—the same kind of faith it required of the boy to let go of the bush and put his trust in God. It is only after we have let go of the bush that we can feel God's power. This is the way it has been in my life. When things have been beyond my control I have turned to the Lord and sought his will, and I have always felt his power and direction in my life.

When I was twelve years old I received my patriarchal blessing. In my blessing the patriarch warned me, "There will be powers about you that would take your life if it were possible, but by living close to the Lord and keeping the Word of Wisdom your life will be spared." I have always felt that the accident in the mission field was one of those times. In fact, for the few days following the accident it seemed as if my life was threatened.

Portales was a small town, and the hospital was inadequate for the surgery I needed. The doctors told dad that if I was not moved by Monday night to Lubbock, Texas, where there was a neurosurgeon, there would be no hope for me because my spinal cord would have been pinched too long. Yet my body had not stabilized, and they dared not move me. It seemed as if there was a stone wall before me. I had to walk by faith; I had to keep a positive outlook and prepare myself to accept the Lord's will—even when it meant walking into the darkness until I hit the wall. It was not until after I had hit the wall that the Lord opened the next door for me. I did not know what he had in store as I lay there and waited those long hours.

Monday evening about an hour before I was to go to Lubbock, the doctors reported that my condition had stabilized, and they thought I could be safely moved. The arrangements were made. Portales had an ambulance service which also served as a hearse. To give me the best service, the ambulance attendants drove up in a new black hearse. The doctors gave me a shot that put me out, and I wore a neck collar so I would not move my head. Crouched down in the back of the ambulance, Dad held my head in his hands between his legs to insure that I would not move. We started out across a hundred miles of desert. About halfway out, the tire on this new ambulance blew out. The ambulance attendants were afraid to jack the car up for fear it might slip off causing more damage to me, so they had to thumb back to town, bring the old ambulance, transfer me into it, and take me to Lubbock.

I barely remember the bright lights in the surgical room, but I can remember hearing the noise as they placed the contraption on my head that was to hold a ten-pound weight in place. Other weights were put on my feet. That night I had fifty pounds of weight pulling my body. The doctors hoped that the weights would stretch my body and put the vertebrae back into place.

In the morning the doctors reported to mom and dad, "It

didn't work. We've done all we can do. Becky is too exhausted now to take her into surgery. If she doesn't have the surgery on her neck by Wednesday, there will be no hope because the spinal cord will have been pinched off too long. The only thing we can do is put her on the surgery schedule. If her condition stabilizes we will operate on her, but the way she is now there is no hope for surgery."

Once again I was left completely in the hands of the Lord. I waited to see his will for me. An hour before my scheduled surgery, my body stabilized and the doctors decided to operate. I have always felt that the hands of the doctors were guided by the Lord as they put the dislocated vertebrae back into place, thus relieving the pressure on the spinal cord.

It's marvelous what the Lord can do. My family wanted to bring me home, but I was in critical condition and had to be moved just as I was on my stryker frame. (A stryker frame is a swivel bed. I would lie two hours on my back, and then the nurses would put a frame on top of me, tighten it down with belts, then turn me over on my stomach and take the top frame off). The commercial airlines would not take me on a regular plane unless I could sit up. It was too long a trip to go by train or bus or any other way. It seemed as if there were no way to bring me back to Salt Lake. I am not sure to this day what happened, but somehow the Utah National Guard heard about my situation, contacted my father, and told him that they flew mercy flights. They were going to fly into the Texas area and would be glad to pick me up and bring me home. It was an answer to our prayers. We had tried so hard to get home; we had exhausted every avenue. And after we had done all we could, the Lord took over.

I will never forget the night the plane came for me. As the nurses pushed me out of the hospital on my stryker frame, I felt the cool, crisp air hit my face. It felt so refreshing and good to me. They put me in the back of an ambulance to take me to the airport. The stryker frame was just a little too long for the ambulance, so the ambulance door did not close tightly in the back. One ambulance attendant was sitting by me, holding in his hand the ten-pound weight that held my neck in place. Mother was up in front with the ambulance driver. The ambulance started to go but as it rounded the first corner my bed started to turn. I did not have a frame on top of me to keep me from falling. I could not move a muscle, but I felt an unseen hand take my arm and, as the bed turned, lift my elbow and place it in the window frame. The ambulance driver gasped, but I said, "It's all right. I've got it. I'll be all right." The ambulance came to a quick stop. The attendants fixed my bed. Someone had forgotten to screw the lock in tightly to keep the bed from turning. Had I not had someone lift my arm and put my elbow in the window frame to stop the turn, I would have turned over, fallen off the frame, and hanged myself.

These are just a few of the life-threatening experiences I had during those days following my accident.

The doctors had told my parents there was no hope for me. I would be nothing more than a vegetable—I would never sit up again, I would never be able to move or walk. They encouraged dad to put me in an institution where I could be taken care of, but somehow this did not seem right to them or to me.

Those early days while I lay on the frame I had time to search my soul, to think about our Father in Heaven and about me and about what I wanted to do with my life. What was left of my life, and what could I do? I could not move one muscle, and yet I knew that God lived. I knew that this had happened for some reason and that somehow the Lord would help me. Because I could feel the closeness of heaven I did not fear, and I knew that I was being watched over and protected.

On Sunday, January 27, 1963, the members of the Valley View Stake fasted for me, and they went to their various ward buildings in the afternoon and had a special prayer in my behalf. Western States missionaries, friends, and family members also fasted for me that Sunday. Sunday evening our stake patriarch came to my hospital room, laid his hands upon my head, and gave me a blessing. He told me, "The day will come when you will stand on your feet, and you will bear witness of the goodness of the Lord in your life."

That is all I needed to hear! A new door was opened for me, and I knew that I would walk. I knew that the day would come when I would stand on my feet. I was very excited. The next morning my index finger wiggled. The people with me that morning and the next few days said they could not see the finger wiggle, but I could feel the muscle tense in the finger. The contraction in the muscle was so weak that it did not move the finger right away, but in a few days those around me could see my finger start to wiggle. Again, I knew there was a God in heaven. I knew there was purpose to my life. And I knew that I would live to see the purpose fulfilled.

In those long hours I lay on the frame, I thought, *I guess I'm not going to be the greatest mother in the world and have a big wonderful family as I have always dreamed. And I guess I will not be the greatest sister missionary in the world and help teach many people and bring the gospel into their lives. What can I be? I do not like to be average. I like to have goals to work for. I like to be something.* Then I decided: *I can be a cripple. I do not know how, but I will learn how to be a cripple, and I will be the greatest cripple who has ever lived.*

Letting go of my own desires and interests, I committed myself into the hands of the Lord, saying, "Father, whatever I have, you can have. I want to do thy will." From then on my life began to change and have new meaning. As I let go of the bush and committed myself to the Lord, I felt a quiet peace and a strength come over me, and I knew I was not alone.

5

The Impossible Takes More Time

There was a sign on the wall in my hospital room that read: The difficult we do at once, the impossible takes more time. It almost seemed like a hopeless task to start from nothing and to regain full use of my physical body. Only one finger would wiggle, but that was a start. The Lord had given me the opportunity, and I would fight back.

I have always been active, full of nervous energy, and have loved to be helping. I suppose this is why being paralyzed is such a good test for me. As I lay in traction those first few months, I realized that I had not changed. My desires and feelings were the same, but my physical ability to do things was gone. It was up to me. What was I going to do with my life? I could lie as a vegetable and slowly die, or I could fight back. It would not be easy to fight. I would get tired of trying. I would get discouraged and frustrated from not being able to do even the simplest thing. But I knew I would once again have the blessing of achievement, and I would be able to taste the joy of success. And in these hours I made my decision: I wanted to work, I wanted to live.

Slowly, very slowly, I made improvement, first wiggling a finger, wiggling and wiggling it so it wouldn't stop. Gradually I began to move my arms. My first task was to pick up a cream-filled cupcake the nurse had laid on my chest and get it into my mouth. It weighed a ton! It fell! But I started over. I had never realized how heavy a cupcake filled with cream could be and how hard it was to lift it. Time and time again it would fall, but I remember the day when I at last got the cupcake to my mouth. It was wonderfully exciting! I was glad I had not stopped. During the next few weeks some of my visitors brought cupcakes to me just so I could do my trick for them. How delightful it was to taste success again!

Being paralyzed can be both frightening and frustrating at times. I can vividly remember my feelings the first night I realized what being paralyzed really meant. I had been confined to the stryker frame nearly twelve weeks, and somehow I had it in my mind that I must lie still or I would fall off. Yet I fully realized that I could not move my fingers or hands because they were paralyzed. The day finally came that I was to be moved off the stryker frame onto a hospital bed. While the doctors and nurses carefully lifted me onto my bed, I thought, *I can hardly wait for them to leave the room, then I will get up.* It seemed to take forever, but finally the last nurse left my room and closed the door behind her. Now it was time for me to get up. I put all my effort into trying to roll over on my right side, but absolutely nothing happened. Not one muscle moved. A cold fear seized me as I whispered, "My gosh, I'm paralyzed." Tears welled up in my eyes and a few rolled off my cheeks onto my pillow. Up until that time I had not fully realized what it meant to be paralyzed. I remember thinking to myself, *It is not going to do any good to cry. I must be very careful that I don't choke.* Once again, the only person I could turn to was my Heavenly Father, so I offered a silent prayer for help. A quiet peace came over me, and without fear I closed my eyes and went to sleep.

Another shock came the next morning when the nurses turned me over on my stomach. I thought I could use my arms since I could lift a cupcake to my mouth, but when I went to move my arms under me and to lift my head off the mattress nothing happened. In fact, if the nurse hadn't noticed and turned my head to the side for me, I could have smothered. I was completely helpless and could not even lift my face out of the mattress.

I am an independent person, and it was hard to get used to being completely helpless. I was dependent upon others for my every need. Simple things such as washing my face, brushing my teeth, turning me over, or feeding me all had to be done for me. But much frustration was taken from me by my family. They had no previous experience with a quadriplegic and the doctors didn't give them much direction, so they just treated me as if I were well. Mother and my sisters helped me with everyday tasks such as bathing, curling and combing my hair, shaving my legs, plucking my eyebrows, and dressing me in stylish clothes. With such devoted care I always felt clean and well groomed—like my old self.

For about the first two years, every time I sat up I would faint. The doctors told mom and dad not to encourage me or give me false hope. I would not be able to sit up again. I would not have full use of my body, and they should not count on anything. In fact, they told mom and dad that if I did not have returned feeling within six to eighteen months, I would not get anymore. One Sunday night getting from the car back into my hospital bed, I fainted seven times. There had not been much return in two years, but I could move my arms a little, bend and straighten my elbows, wiggle my finger, and help someone turn me over. Yet I knew that I would walk. I also knew that I was endeavoring to do an impossible thing, but that Heavenly Father would help me because he had made the promise to me.

I had thought paralyzed people were stiff, but from firsthand experience I knew I was as wiggly as a wet noodle. I was limber and could move in any direction. From just below the neck to my toes I could not feel anything. My sensations were gone. You could have cut off my arms and legs, and I would not feel a thing.

Once while in the hospital I had an infection which caused a strange coldness inside me and kept me awake, so I asked for a hot water bottle. The nurse filled one with hot water from the tap and wrapped it in a big towel. I knew I had to be careful, so I laid it up by my head, placed my hands on the nice warm towel, and relaxed. The sleeping pill must have taken effect, for some time later I awoke with the impression that my arm was being burned. Drowsy from the sleeping pill, I pushed the hot water bottle out of the bed and went back to sleep. The hot water bottle did not fall to the floor, but instead slipped down between my arms where I couldn't feel it. The next morning when the nurse came in, I had second-degree burns on my arms and hands. I still carry a scar on my arm; and every time I see it, it reminds me to wake up, listen and heed the promptings of the still small voice.

My body's temperature control system has not worked since I became paralyzed. If I go out on a hot day my body heats up, and before long I get dizzy and tired and go into heat exhaustion. In cold weather I do not feel a thing, but my teeth start to chatter; and if I'm not careful, my feet can get frostbite. Like a hot house plant, I have to stay within moderate temperatures.

I can still remember the triumph and excitement I felt as I sat up for the first time. I was at home on a full bed, rolling over by throwing my left arm across my body. This time my arm went farther than usual, and I was nearly on my right side with my right shoulder under me. I struggled to pull my right arm farther under me, and slowly I inched my arms forward until I could reach a point and straighten my elbows and raise the top part of my body up to a forward sitting position. I was weak, tired, and shaky, but I was sitting up with all the weight resting on my two arms in front of me. My family cheered at my victory—it was a first.

There are no words that begin to express my love and deep appreciation to the doctors, nurses, therapist, and all those who helped me in those early days. The nurses helped me to learn to feed myself by taping a spoon in my left hand. What a thrill to be just a wee bit more independent and accomplish another skill! The eight months I spent at the hospital in Salt Lake prepared me for greater success at the rehabilitation center in Roy, Utah.

Whatever can I do at occupational therapy? I wondered, as the nurse pushed my wheelchair down the hall and into a large, bright room filled with long tables and elderly patients working on different projects. All fear and anxiety left me when I met Gwen, the occupational therapist, and in no time at all she had me doing crafts. Each project became more challenging and the rewards of joy more intense.

The first day I painted a simple design on a dish towel. Gwen had secured the dish towel with thumb tacks onto a large tile used for ceilings. I held the tube of paint in my left hand and used my right hand to guide the tip along the lines, resting the weight of my body on my arms, which put extra stress on them. After some practice, I was able to make the paint run smoothly and to see the design come alive with color. I was very proud. I had done it myself and I would give it to mother on her birthday. Tears of joy ran down mother's face as she opened the package and looked at the dish towel. I thought that perhaps mother would be the only one who would appreciate the great effort I had put forth, but after several months of practice I received two blue ribbons at the state fair for pictures I had painted.

It was Gwen who took the time to work with me until she came up with a gadget to tape in my left hand that would hold a pencil so I could learn to write again. Using mostly jerky shoulder movement, I began the tedious project of learning to write. My first letters were big and awkward; but as the months passed by I developed more strength and better balance. Gradually I was able to hold a pencil in my own hand with the aid of two hoops of masking tape which slid over my index finger and thumb, making it possible for me to apply pressure on the pencil. Once again success followed work and practice.

"I am going to walk and I want braces!" I told the physical therapists in January of 1964. I could feel their hesitance—I knew they didn't think I would walk again. My first braces were a pair of black suede shoes fastened to metal supports that came up to my armpits, with leather straps at strategic points to hold my legs and body straight. It took a couple of therapists about twenty minutes to get me buckled into my braces. They tied straps on the back of my braces and secured them to hooks on the ceiling; then if I fell, I would just swing and not injure myself.

What an experience for me to stand in the parallel bars! I wasn't able to feel the weight of my body on my feet or even the little movements I made. I couldn't grasp the bars because my hands were paralyzed. All I could do was balance and look down and say, "Yes, this is me! This is me!" and I would wiggle and try and try.

One afternoon while in braces I was standing in the parallel bars. There was an older man who was recovering from a stroke working at the other end of the bars. "Come on, Charlie, you can do it," the therapist said, encouraging him to stand up by holding onto the bars.

"No," replied the old man.

"Sure you can," coached the therapist. "You stood up this morning by yourself."

"No, I don't want to," the man flatly stated.

"Why?" asked the therapist.

To this question he replied, "Look what's coming at me."

Somehow I felt like a real monster, but I couldn't help laughing out loud at his cute response.

It was at this point in my recovery that the Lord sent Wendell, another therapist, to help me. If Wendell thought I wasn't going to get well, he didn't tell me. All he said was, "You can do better tomorrow than you're doing today." I knew I could too. I could not do worse. I had to do better. Wendell cut my braces down to my waist. It took me almost a year to learn to balance myself over my legs. Then he cut my braces down to the tops of my legs. It took me about three years to learn to keep my hips under me.

Most of the time as I worked, it seemed as if I were going backwards, as if I got worse instead of better. But I kept struggling and I kept working. I came home from the rehabilitation center in the fall of 1964, and Wendell would come three times a week to the house to give me physical therapy. I appreciated his willingness to help me, his faith in me, and his desire to help me get well. I worked hard, and little by little I could see a change. But even after I noticed a small change in a muscle or a feeling, it seemed to take years before I would see improvement in my ability to use that muscle.

In September 1966, Grandpa Reeve came to live with us. Every day he would put up my parallel bars, put on my braces, and stand me up so I could walk. At first grandpa would have to help me move my legs with each step, but gradually I was able to balance my body and move my feet on my own. The work was slow and it seemed to drain me of all my strength and energy, but I was determined to walk again. From the first time I stood up in my braces, I spent many hours just trying to balance and then to move. After I reached a certain point, the therapists would cut off my braces and I would have to start over.

It was January 3, 1968, just a little over six years since I had been hurt. This day I experienced a peculiar feeling in my hips and back, and somehow I knew that I could stand and walk and that my hips would take the weight of my body so that my arms wouldn't have to support all the weight. When Wendell came that night to give me physical therapy, he put my braces on me and stood me up in the walker. Up until this time I had been able to walk only a few feet until my arms would tire and give out from holding all the weight of my body. When I reached this point Wendell would pull the wheelchair behind me, and I would sit down.

I had never tried to go out of my room or maneuver the walker before. But this night my hips supported my weight. When I started to walk, I felt so good that when I reached the door I kept going. I walked out of my room, down the hall, and into the front room. I turned around about two-thirds of the way into the front room and walked back into my bedroom. It was about thirty feet in all. I knew Wendell was surprised. He had offered to bring my wheelchair behind me, but I knew I could make it. I wish I could describe the excitement I felt. I had been working toward this day for six years!

Perhaps only I will appreciate the overwhelming joy I felt the night I actually took my first steps. But for those moments when I walked into the front room, I felt it was worth all the time, effort, and work that I had put forth. I will be eternally grateful to my Father in Heaven who blessed me so that I could reach that point. How glad I was that I had not given up because someone said, "It can't be done"! Impossible things just take more time.

6

You Can Trust the Lord

As a young girl I had exciting and wonderful dreams about going on a date. I used to imagine that when my date came for me I would be dressed up in a beautiful dress and have had my hair done at a beauty shop. I pictured in my mind that I would walk down all the stairs (like you see in the movies) when my date came to get me. Well, I don't know where I got the stairs from—our front room doesn't have one stair in it. But that didn't matter. I would still dream about the time when I would go on a date and what I would look like.

But dreams are different from reality. Not long after my accident I was lying in the hospital on a stryker frame. My head had been shaved about two months before, and the hair had started to grow back. But instead of beautiful hair, I had stubs. My eyebrows, well, I had not been able to pluck them for several months so I had the one-brow look. On the stryker frame as I lay on my stomach, a cloth mask supported my head. The mask went across the top of my forehead and across my chin and up the sides of my cheeks, leaving my nose and mouth free to breathe and eat. When the nurses turned me over on my back, I had "puffed face" from lying on that mask.

The worst thing of all was that I had gone for two months without brushing my teeth. The nurses would brush them a little bit while I lay on the frame, but they were careful about putting water in my mouth because I couldn't sit up and couldn't cough up water if any got down my throat. I really had dragon breath. And instead of a beautiful fancy dress, I wore a wrinkled hospital gown with a white sheet covering me.

One December morning a nurse came into the room and said, "Good morning. How are you this morning, Becky?"

"Fine," I responded.

"We're going to make Christmas tree decorations today," she announced.

"Oh, good," I replied, wondering how I was going to make decorations without being able to move.

The nurse turned me upside down on my stryker frame so that I was face down looking at the floor, and pushed my bed down the hall. When I got to the big room, I could smell a Christmas tree. A record player was playing Christmas carols, and handicapped children were making decorations. The nurse gave mother a cardboard box cut in the shape of a star which she was supposed to cover with tin foil. That would be my decoration. Everyone seemed to be having such a good time when all of a sudden the room got very quiet. *I hope no one is here to see me,* I thought. Just then from under the frame by my head appeared another big head saying "Hi!" There was the face of a returned missionary, looking into my face.

"Hi!" I answered, being careful that my dragon breath would not get all over him.

"Oh, Becky, it looks like you've got company," the nurse remarked. "Let's take you back to your room and turn you up so that you can visit with him."

No, you don't have to do that, I thought, but she, not hearing my thoughts, pushed me back to the room and turned me up so that I could visit.

What a humbling experience! There I lay with puffed face

and dragon breath, talking to Ken, one of my old supervising elders. He had heard of my accident and had come to visit me. I tried not to look at him right in the eyes as we talked and laughed about some of our mission experiences. I kept thinking, *Well, any time he'll go now.* As he got ready to leave he asked, "Can I come back and see you?"

I thought, *My gosh, whatever turns you on,* as I mumbled, "Yes."

Within the week he was back to see me. The second time he came I had a unique experience. As he walked into my room there was a special spirit about him, and it seemed as if our spirits communicated. Instantly I felt comfortable and close to him. I enjoyed his visit. Within a month, he asked me to marry him.

When I was up leaping around, I couldn't get a date. But here I was confined to bed, unable to move a muscle, and someone wanted to marry me. It seemed unreal. At this time Patriarch Williams gave me a blessing in which he said, "The day will come when you will stand on your feet and bear witness of the goodness of the Lord in your life." I figured that I would be made well soon. Besides, I didn't know of any disease that lasted longer than six months, so I told Ken I would marry him. For the next three years Ken and I shared many hopes, dreams and disappointments, and much happiness and sorrow together.

Most of our courting was done in the hospital. Ken would go to school during the week, and on the weekends he would visit me. He would hitchhike, drive up, or come any way he could, but he would faithfully come. Almost every day for three years I got a letter from him. These were not the mushy kind of letters. They were faith-filled letters that would say, "Becky, trust the Lord. Get in and work hard so that we can be married." And then he would tell me what he was doing. These letters meant a lot to me, and mother would read them to me every day when they came. I could not write back, so mother would write to Ken for me each day. I would tell her what to write. After a while I was able to train myself to write left-handed, and I could write my own letters.

As the three years drew to a close, Ken was about to graduate from BYU. We had set six different wedding dates, but none of them seemed to work out. After each one we would postpone the date and wait a while for my physical health to improve. We had fasted many times during the three years, and we had prayed continually that the Lord might grant the desires of our hearts.

I can remember one particular Sunday that Ken brought me home from Sunday School. I was tired, and so he laid me down on my bed. He had to go back to Provo, but he knelt down and offered a prayer before he left. I do not remember all the words he said, but I can remember the spirit of the prayer. He told Heavenly Father how much we loved each other and how hard we had worked so that we could be together. But he said, "Father, we will do thy will. We just need to know thy will for us." As he concluded we both hugged each other, and tears streamed down our faces. We must have felt that our desires might not be granted. After he left I lay on the bed, and I could feel pain right in the middle of my heart. *This must be what a broken heart feels like, I thought. This must be a little like how the Savior felt.* I prayed to God, and the pain went away.

Ken went home to spend Thanksgiving with his family, and I spent the holiday with mine. That night I was tired and went to bed early. Calling dad to my side I said, "I can't sleep tonight. Would you give me a blessing?" He laid his hands on my head, and with the power of the holy priesthood he gave me a blessing that I would relax and rest. As he was closing the blessing he added, "In an unexpected way in the near future, you will see the hand of the Lord in your behalf." I had never heard anything like that before, and I pondered those words all night long. I thought, *The most unexpected thing that could happen to me is that I would get well and get married.*

I was excited. I called Ken the next day and told him of my feelings and thoughts. That Christmas he gave me a diamond ring but our joy and excitement was not to last long. Within two months I had given my ring back—our engagement was over. This truly was a most unexpected change and it took the hand of the Lord to bring it about. Several weeks before this I had decided that maybe I did need to know what he wanted us to do. So I decided to fast and pray once more. I had barely started to open my fast with prayer when for the second time in my life a small voice came directly into my mind saying, "It is not time yet. This is the way the Lord wants it."

I have never had such a direct answer so I thanked the Lord for the answer and then asked him to give me courage to do what he wanted done. The hardest thing I have ever had to do is to let my sweetheart go and watch my hopes and dreams once again dashed to pieces. I told myself, *I know I can trust the Lord. And if the Lord gives a commandment he will open up the way for it to happen, just as he did for Nephi. I know that he answered our prayers, and I know he will help us. If I am going to trust him with all of my heart, I will let go of the bush and I will not cry and make a fuss, but I will be full of faith and will lean upon the Lord.* That is exactly what I did, and I learned a great lesson through this experience. I learned without a shadow of a doubt that *you can trust the Lord.* Yes, every cell in my body knows that *you can trust the Lord.* I could not have done such a thing by myself, but I didn't have to. The Lord blessed me and gave me the strength.

Perhaps a comparison will explain how the Lord helps. Has the dentist ever drilled and fixed your teeth without first having given you a shot to deaden the pain? When the air or water hits the nerve, you can feel pain. But if the dentist gives you a shot to freeze your mouth, you feel no pain. You go through the same experience, but you do not feel the pain. That is the way it was with me. I put my life in the Lord's hands. I committed myself to him. I did not make a fuss and just sit around. I did the best I could. When I got lonesome and discouraged, I would reach up to my Father and he would bless me. He carried much of the pain, and I was only inconvenienced for a while. I knew I had been blessed of the Lord. There is no bitterness in my heart; instead, there is an overwhelming gratitude to our Father in Heaven for giving me a friend such as Ken.

7

When One Door Closes

Sometimes I wish life would stay just as it is, but that is not possible. The old saying "Life is a journey, not a camp" is true. After you go through one set of experiences, the doors close on those experiences and the particular challenges that went with them: you are then ready for different experiences. I have found that as one door closes, another door is opening. This has been my experience time and time again. One door will close, but many more will open. With new experiences come new opportunities for growth, new friends and new challenges.

After I came home from the rehabilitation center, many opportunities came into my life to give me new challenges to overcome. I was called to be the editor of our ward newspaper. Each week we would put out a four-page paper which would announce coming events and give interesting, eventful news about ward members. I served in this position for nearly eight years. There were sometimes as many as thirty people working under me, including typists, folders, printers, and writers. This call took much of my time.

During this time mother was managing thirty sales girls for a lingerie company. This gave both mother and me an opportunity to do something together in the home, and it helped me gain new experiences. I called the sales girls on the phone to check on their sales, answered their questions, and answered the phone when mother went away. On several occasions I even went out and held house parties when mother was unable to make it. I enjoyed the challenge of meeting the public and working with them.

A man who hired handicapped people to call about stolen checks offered me a job. It was my responsibility to call each store listed on a sheet as soon as I could and alert the store not to accept these stolen checks. I enjoyed this opportunity during the five years I worked for this service; but as time passed, I was ready for new experiences. I knew there must be something more to my life than dialing a phone.

I had attended BYU in Provo for two years prior to my mission. My major was elementary education. I thought to myself, *Why not finish and be a schoolteacher?* Feeling good about my decision, I announced that I was going back to school to become a teacher. When I told people about my plans, I could feel from their response whether or not they thought I could make it. I must admit I didn't look much like a teacher. I was still weak and often fainted when I sat up. I had just learned to write left-handed. I would not be able to go into the classroom in this condition. But I had the name of the man I was supposed to call, and I telephoned the BYU Salt Lake Center and asked for Keith Smith. When he answered, I asked, "Can you help me?" Then I proceeded to explain my situation. I made only one telephone call, and through Keith Smith the Lord opened a door that permitted me, since I was too weak to attend class, to have BYU instructors come to my house.

I feel a great love for each teacher who helped me to graduate. I would take only one class at a time. Perhaps the professors had to go more slowly than normal, but somehow I was able to complete the class. Then I would sign up for another one, and then another one. It was exciting to be able to learn again and to feel that I was accomplishing something. The teachers were interested in me and would help me if I would just put forth the effort to do the work. And the harder I worked, the greater became my strength and ability.

The day finally came when I was strong enough to go into a classroom situation. My first class, a media class for elementary education, was held at a high school. This was a challenging situation for me. Not only was it the first time I had actually gone out into a classroom situation on my own, but also I was not able to take my electric wheelchair to class. (It can't be folded up and we had no van in which to transport it.)

My electric wheelchair is so easy to control that when I am in it I don't even feel as if I am paralyzed. It is heavy, and I can maneuver it easily without its tipping over. I drive it with my right hand, and that leaves my left hand free to do other things. As I went to this class, I left my electric wheelchair behind and went in my lightweight chair. Now, as a paralyzed person if I sit up and hold both arms straight out in front of me, I tip over each time, because I don't have the stomach or back muscles to hold my body upright. Every time I push the lightweight wheelchair forward, the momentum pushes my head forward and the rest of my body follows. So here I was in my lightweight chair, and about every time I tried to make the chair go, it felt as if I were falling out on my head.

I went into this classroom not knowing if I could take care of my own needs and problems, but through the Lord's help I was able to go. I felt great satisfaction in this media class because the teachers let me do all the things I could for myself. And when the task was beyond my physical ability, they would help me. I found that I was able to do most assignments by myself.

After finishing the media class, I was able to go on to the next class on my own. I took only one class at a time because that was all the homework I could handle. I was still editor of the ward paper and spoke to various groups as they would call me, and these activities took most of my time and energy.

You do not have to be paralyzed very long to realize that a paralyzed person does not go to school alone. Actually the degree should have been shared with my mother. She is the one who would have to arrange her schedule to get me up and dressed, take me to classes, and see that all my needs were met. She would run to the library to get the books and do everything else that needed to be done. Mother was always cheerful; never once did she act tired, disappointed, exhausted, or in any other way to make me feel as if she did not want to help. She earned the degree with me.

It took me eight years to finish my last two years of school but I didn't care how long it took. I was excited about it. Self-motivation comes easy to me; and because I have always wanted to excel, I didn't have to be coaxed to study. Many friends helped me. If I had to have any art drawings, I always called Rachael to help me with my assignment. Nancy helped me with new math, and Kelly pulled me through physics. Mary accompanied me when we took two classes together. She would sit in class with me and push me to the next class, helping with books, assignments, and note taking when I got tired. How grateful I am to everyone—my teachers, my family, and my friends—who helped me!

When the time came for me to do student teaching, I didn't know how I was going to handle it. Up to this time when I became overly tired one day, I would be down in bed a couple of days just to get my strength back. With the pressure and stress of school I was more susceptible to kidney infection, and it seemed as if I spent most of my time in bed sick. I was not sure exactly how I would be able to student teach, yet I could wait no longer. I had to student teach the fall of 1973 because BYU was going to change its teaching program, and the new program would be more difficult for me. The semester before I started my student teaching, I enrolled in two classes which met every Tuesday and Thursday. I decided that this would be a good chance to see if I could sit up and work extra long hours. Tuesday night I went to my first class and then to the second class. I came home and literally dropped into bed. I didn't get up again until Thursday, just before my classes. Once again I attended the two classes, came home exhausted, and went to bed. I didn't get out of bed until the next Tuesday. I wondered how I would be able to student teach. I would have to go every day. I forced the fears and doubts out of my mind, knowing the Lord would help me if I was supposed to do it.

September fourth came. Mother woke me about 5:00 A.M. She gave me my bath and dressed me, got me in my wheelchair, and drove me to Provo. I sat in my first teaching class until noon. Then mother brought me home and put me to bed. I did my homework on the bed. The next morning the same thing happened; in fact, I was able to go to school every day for nearly three months and accomplish everything I was supposed to do. It was indeed a miracle, and again I knew that God hears and answers prayers.

My first student teaching assignment was at the Edgemont Elementary School in Sandy, Utah. The principal, Mr. King, assured me that everything would work out fine and that the staff and children were looking forward to having me. What a great feeling to know that others cared! He assigned me to work with Mrs. Mitchell, a first-grade teacher. "You'll just love her," he said. "She is looking forward to helping you." I put forth my very best effort in my student teaching. Dad would drive me to Sandy every morning before work and get me settled. If he couldn't take me right to my desk, there was always a pair of hands to help me up the stairs and into my classroom. I appreciated the training and experience I received under Mrs. Mitchell. My first teaching situation was positive. I loved my class—they had to be the cutest class of first graders ever. I was assigned to do a unit on weather, and I was expected to perform at my best. My coordinator from BYU was so kind and anxious for me to have this student teaching experience that she arranged for me to teach only a half-day, which was all my strength would allow.

A marvelous thing happened in my second teaching situation. I stayed at Edgemont Elementary School and worked under Mr. Jarrett, the resource teacher. My coordinator at BYU thought it would be good for me to work in a resource area where there were children with learning disabilities and other problems. I felt satisfaction in being able to teach children with learning disabilities. It seemed as if I had a special "in" with them because I too was handicapped, and they recognized it and trusted me. I could help them more easily. And again I was able to go every day.

After I had finished my student teaching, but before I could graduate from BYU, I had to take a few more classes. I took a heavy load spring and summer to fulfill the requirements. I attended the 1974 BYU graduation, and when the officials handed me my teaching certificate I knew without a doubt that there was a God in heaven. I knew that doors had been opened for me as they were needed in order that I might accomplish what I did. Friends had been raised up, teachers had been raised up, opportunities had been raised up, and I was able to complete my goal.

Following graduation, I wanted to do something special for all those people who had made it possible for me to graduate. I wanted it to be something of me, something I did, something that I had to sacrifice a little to do. I did not have enough money to buy them all presents—there were too many people involved. But as I lay in bed one night the idea came to send them each a special thank-you note. I would create my own design. I asked our neighbor to take a picture of me in my cap and gown. Then I had it printed on a thank-you note, leaving a space for me to write. I wrote, folded, secured with a seal, addressed, and mailed over five hundred hand-written thank-you notes. It took time and great effort to form each word, but I wrote each word with love and deep appreciation. These notes enabled me to give something of myself to those who had helped me achieve. When people say that Becky Reeve has graduated from BYU, I smile to myself and think, *Yes, I sat on the stand and took the diploma, but I wrote over five hundred thank-you notes to people who made it possible.*

One of the great honors paid to me the day of my graduation was the presence of my beloved cousin John Reeve. John hitchhiked all night from the Tetons in Wyoming to make it in time. Over many years we had shared a close relationship. He told me he would never miss my graduation.

All my family got together—from far and near—at my graduation. We had a Rex Reeve Round-up in Springville, Utah, because my older brother, Rex, Jr., was getting his Ph.D. degree the same day I was getting my B.S. What a special day it was in my life!

Another door had closed behind me, but I was eager for new experiences. The next door that opened gave me the opportunity to tutor students in my home. What a thrill to help someone else! How exciting to feel self-worth again and to know that through my efforts I was in a position to help someone else. No greater joy can come than when you bend down and lift someone else up. I loved the students I tutored, and I will be eternally grateful that I was able to have this experience because of the great joy and satisfaction I received.

8

My Cup Runneth Over

What could be greater than this? I had graduated from BYU and I loved tutoring my students. I was happy with life, hoping that it would never change. But life is full of changes. A change was to come into my life that turned out to be one of the greatest blessings I have ever had.

One January afternoon in 1975 dad and mother had an appointment to meet with the First Presidency. That is always a humbling experience (even for the family); we all wondered what the Brethren wanted. When dad and mother returned home, they told me they had been asked to preside over a mission. I was ecstatic. Mom and dad were going to take me with them into the mission field. I never thought I would get a second chance. When dad and mother accepted the call, they didn't know where they would be sent. They had to wait just like every other missionary for the call to come. It could be anywhere in the whole world, but that didn't matter to me. I was so pleased that it was hard to keep the secret, and it was hard to keep from smiling. I smiled all the time inside because I was filled with such joy.

One night as I lay on my bed in my room, I poured out my heart to my Father in Heaven to express my gratitude. I was happy for an opportunity to go back into the mission field, and I wanted to thank him. It seemed as if I had no sooner got started than doubts came into my mind. *Becky, why are you so happy? What if you are sent to an area that does not have the facilities to fix your electric wheelchair and it breaks down? Oh, my gosh,* I thought, *that is a possibility.* It's hard to find someone who knows how to fix electric wheelchairs. *What if we go across the seas and no one can fix it? What will I do?* The next thought that flashed into my mind was, *What if you need a doctor? Where will you get medical help?* It seemed as if I spent more days down than up with various infections. My doctor had been a great help to me, and I hated to leave his influence and his direction. The third thought that came to me was, *What if your mother and father are called to a big mission, and they have to travel a lot? Who will take care of you? I don't know,* I thought.

And then I said out loud, "Becky, you are surely stupid. Satan, you get away from me. I will not listen to you. I do not have to and I will not. Bug someone else, because I will not listen." I turned to my Father in Heaven and I simply said, "Father, I don't have much left that wiggles, but what I have you can have; and I want to go on this mission more than anything else in the world. I don't care if I have to lie in a room somewhere on a bed and can never even sit up because my wheelchair is broken. I want to go." After I had made this commitment, the sweetest, most peaceful feeling saturated my being; and I knew that God would take care of us.

And take care of us he did. He sent us to the California, Anaheim Mission. That has to be the greatest wheelchair mission in the world. It seemed to me that there were wheelchair fix-it shops on almost every corner, about as plentiful as gas stations. And interestingly enough, right across from the mission home lived Doctor Sanders, a urologist who had been trained by my doctor at the University of Utah. Every time I needed medicine I would call him, and he would bring it over to the mission home. I didn't have to wait five minutes in a doctor's office.

In addition the mission area was small. Even though there were a lot of people in the mission, the farthest point from our mission home was only two and a half hours away, which meant that every night mother and dad could be home to take care of me.

The members in California were super. I grew to love them with all of my heart. I cannot think of one bad experience. The people were kind and gracious and warm as they welcomed us to California.

The mission home was beautiful, with a sliding glass door that I could drive out of. I could do wheelies in any of the rooms of the mission home. A ramp was built the first day I got there by our neighbors; and I could drive down the ramp and around the driveway in the shade of the beautiful trees, or I could go anywhere I wanted on the block. We were only five minutes away from church, which made it easy for my companions to take me to church.

I had the special blessing of companions while I was in the mission field. Mother was in charge of the mission home and the meals. We didn't have a housekeeper or a cook, but we had asked some of my cousins to stay with us for a certain length of time to help. My cousin Evelyn and my sister JoAnn went with us to help us get started. We had lots of experiences together. I felt as if I had been let out of a cage. Here I was riding with a companion on a freeway. I had never done anything like this before in my whole life.

I can remember once going to the San Diego Mission when President and Sister Bradshaw had invited me down to speak at the sisters' conference. Evelyn and I had a great time as we drove alone to San Diego. We had the written directions as to which turn-off we should take, but we had no idea where we were going. What a thrill and a triumph to find we had made it!

My next companion was my cousin Sherrie. It was with Sherrie that I learned to communicate better and to express my feelings. Sherrie had a beautiful alto voice, and we loved to sing together. I had a squeaky little voice but she kept encouraging me, so we would sing when we were in the car or wherever we had the opportunity. I got so that I could carry a tune.

After Sherrie left, my sixteen-year-old niece Cory, who was in her junior year at high school, came out for the summer months. Cory and I have always shared a special bond of love. We shared a room together, and at night as we lay in bed we would share our feelings, thoughts, hopes, and desires. She had a lot of natural ability in taking care of me. She could handle me well. When we picked up Cory from the airport she was crying because she was leaving her boyfriend behind, and she never thought two months would pass. But she got right in, forgot herself, went to work, and fell in love with the mission. When we were ready to say good-bye to her, she was crying again—this time because she was leaving and she could not believe the two months were up.

My next companion was Deanna. What a joy and a pleasure it was to be with her! We got along very well. I was a little bit nervous, being so much older than Deanna, who had just graduated from high school, but Deanna was mature beyond her years. She would sing alto and I would sing soprano, and we would sing together wherever we went. At Christmastime we wanted to do something special for our families. Deanna had fourteen brothers and sisters, and I had my family that I wanted to remember. We got pieces of wood, sanded them, and decoupaged pictures or sayings onto them. We had lots of fun doing this together, and somehow we finished, wrapped, and mailed all of them before she went home.

As each companion left, I had an empty spot in my heart; for I had grown close to each girl and hated to see her go. Kathleen Kay, a cousin from mother's side of the family, spent the last six months with us. We called her K. K. It was not hard to love her; she had a warm and bubbly personality. While I was with K. K., dad was called to be a General Authority. At the close of our mission, just a month before we were ready to go home, mother had a heart attack. Up to this time mother had taken care of my needs, and the girls would dress me, take me places, and be with me. Now K. K. had to take care of me all by herself. I knew that she could do it; I had no fears because I had confidence in her. Great bonds of love grew between us as she took total care of me, doing the many things for me that I could not do for myself.

The mission was wonderful. We were not far away, so our other family members could come and visit us. When JoAnn came, she would always make sure that I had an enjoyable time and saw new things. Each time the family came, I went sight-seeing with them around California. I went to Disneyland, Marine Land, the wax museum, and many other places. I had never had experiences like these before. Yes, I loved California. I loved the weather. I loved the members. The gospel was just as true in California as it was in the Western States Mission and in Utah. While in the mission home we were able to friendship and teach some wonderful people and to see them join the Church. What a thrill it was to see the gospel come into their lives!

I suppose the thing I loved most about the mission was the missionaries. I was old enough to be their mother and I did not have any children of my own, so I claimed all these wonderful missionaries. It seemed that since Heavenly Father had sent them to California, Anaheim Mission, they were part mine too. I did all I could to help them and to strengthen them. Before each missionary came out into the mission field, we would get a picture of him, and a pink piece of paper with information about him. It was so exciting to look at the picture and read the information and to know that a new missionary was coming to join us in building the kingdom.

The missionaries came from many different backgrounds. We had some from broken homes, some from member homes, and some from homes in which the parents had told them not to come back if they went on missions. We had a blind elder, a deaf elder, and elders with health problems. We had elders called to this mission and elders who had been transferred to this mission, but it did not matter where they came from or what their problems were. I loved them and so did mom and dad. And we worked together as a team. Their first day in the mission field was spent at the mission home. Mom would fix them lunch, and then we would have an orientation meeting while dad interviewed each missionary. I felt each missionary's spirit as I heard him bear his testimony. I knew the anticipation he felt in his heart when he was assigned to his first companion.

To spend the first day in the mission field with the new missionaries was always a thrill. As they bore their testimony that first day, I would think, *Yes, you would be a great stake president. You could be an elder's quorum president. You would make a wonderful mother.* I would try to visualize each missionary as he could be. Mothers see their children grow physically—take their first steps, cut their first tooth, and say their first words; but I got to see my great missionary sons and daughters grow spiritually. As they would get in and forget themselves, be obedient to the rules, and follow the counsel of their priesthood leaders, marvelous things would happen in their lives. They would become powerful. During each zone conference I attended, I listened to the missionaries bear their testimonies. It was not so much what they said that convinced me of their progress; I could feel by the Spirit that they were obedient and that they had grown. I would think, *Yes, he (or she) has grown this month, or he is ready to be a district leader now. He is ready to be a zone leader, or he could be a senior companion.*

I learned a lot about priesthood leadership in those three years by observing missionaries in leadership positions. I was able to associate closely with dad's assistants, men who were like unto Nephi and Alma. No hour was too long for the assistants; they wholeheartedly completed every assignment. "I have to be careful what I ask the assistants to do," dad told me, "because they will do it." If they couldn't complete it they would die trying. (In fact, I thought more than once that they were going to wear themselves out because they were so dedicated.)

When missionaries were ready to go home, mom would fix a lovely meal for them. After the meal we would have a farewell meeting. It was a humbling experience to attend these meetings and to feel the spirit that accompanied missionaries who had served with all their hearts and had learned to find the Lord. Tears would run down my face, and I would think as each bore his last testimony in the field, *Yes, you can go now. I cannot do anything more to help you. I have done all I could in these two years to strengthen you and to teach you what I know. You know how to find the Lord and to get answers to your problems.* They were not the same missionaries who had come out. This time as they testified, they were men and women of God; and when they spoke, they spoke with the power and authority of God.

When I was younger, with my overwhelming desire to be a mother, I wanted about fifteen or twenty children. Now, I have over six hundred fifty of the greatest missionary sons and daughters anyone could ever ask for. I love each one of them; and since our Father in Heaven sent them to the mission while we were there, they became part of me. As long as there is breath in my body, I will be interested in my missionaries. (I have planned a missionary reunion about seventy years down the road in the celestial kingdom, and all my missionaries and their mates and families are supposed to be there.) And what a joyous occasion it will be when we all meet together!

I hope and pray that, wherever my missionaries are and whatever they do, they will always be worthy servants of our Father in Heaven. I pray that they will stand as witnesses for Jesus Christ at all times and in all places; that the sisters will be worthy mothers and the elders will be worthy priesthood leaders in their homes; that they will strengthen their immediate families; and because of the great abilities they have been blessed with, that they will reach out and strengthen others.

You cannot get into the Lord's debt. There is absolutely no way you can. Little did I know when my first mission was cut short that I would have the choice experience of going on another mission. I attended hundreds of meetings where I felt the Holy Spirit. I listened to thousands of testimonies and shared numerous experiences of loving, caring, and sacrificing. Truly these were three choice years of my life. How thankful I am that I could have this experience! My cup is so full that it runneth over.

9

Happiness Comes from Within

If you are searching for happiness, look within yourself. I believe you can be as happy as you want to be in any circumstance you may find yourself, because the key to happiness is locked inside your heart. Happiness is an attitude—it is the way we look at life and the way we look at ourselves. We all like to be around positive, cheerful people who are filled with faith and are working toward a goal. Happiness may be found in a room, a flower, a friend, or an experience. If we take the time to enjoy the world around us, we can find happiness; and the memories of these experiences can be a source of joy forever.

I had never taken medicine in my life, and my body was not used to the pain-killing drugs the nurses gave me while I was in intensive care following surgery on my broken neck. I would come to for a brief period and then would go back to sleep.

One day when I was conscious, I overheard a nurse talking about the upcoming marriage of her daughter. I wanted to explain to the nurse our concept of temple marriage, but I was not conscious long enough.

Visiting hours were five minutes every two hours, and when dad came in to visit me I aroused and said, "Sound the trumps."

"Not right now," he quietly replied, while standing in a room of critically ill patients.

"Sound the trumps," I said again. I had a talk I needed to give on temple marriage.

"No," dad embarrassedly replied, trying to calm me.

"Sound the trumps," I ordered.

"No, not now," dad responded.

"Well, then, stand back and I will. Da da da dum da dum. Da da da dum da dum. Da da da dum da dum," I shouted for the third time at the top of my voice. But after exerting all my energy I was too tired to give my important talk on temple marriage, and I fell back asleep.

If you can sell paralysis, you can sell anything.

While I was staying in the rehabilitation division of the Weber Memorial Hospital I had an English roommate, fifty-two-year-old Lilian, who was recuperating from serious back surgery which had left her left leg partially paralyzed. After dinner we stayed in our room and practiced some of the techniques we had learned that day. Usually on Wednesday evenings a young girl volunteering as a candy striper would visit us until her folks came to pick her up.

This particular Wednesday night I had decided to practice a transfer from the wheelchair onto the bed. I worked hard for quite a while until finally I got both legs straight forward on the bed then, while sitting in my wheelchair, I brought it up as close to the bed as I could. Now I was ready to begin my transfer. As I started to push myself out of the chair straight onto the bed, my wheelchair started to move backwards. Lilian, seeing my situation, said, "Just a minute, and I will hold your chair." She grabbed her crutches and hobbled across the room. With her crutches still under her arms, she braced the chair. Once again I tried to get onto the bed. This time the chair stayed in place, but the bed started slipping away from me.

What a sight! My legs were on the bed, my hands were still balancing on the wheelchair, and my body was slipping down between the wheelchair and the bed. There was nothing left to do but laugh. And laugh we did, until tears were streaming down our faces. Amid all this laughter the young candy striper asked, "Is it more fun to be paralyzed or normal?"

Sea World was an overwhelming experience for me—the grounds and setting are beautiful, the hired help are clean-cut and considerate, and a wheelchair is welcomed. I enjoyed watching all the animals perform, but my favorite was Shamu, the killer whale. He was nineteen feet long and weighed fifty-three hundred pounds, and yet he was as graceful as a ballerina in the water. It was hard for me to believe that anyone could train a whale to jump thirty feet out of the water and to perform many other complicated tricks. He was striking with his black and white coloring, and I fell in love with this elegant creature. I attended Shamu's performance at least twice every time I went to Sea World (and I went to Sea World about six times). I even hung a poster of Shamu in my bedroom.

"This is the last time you will be able to go to Sea World before dad and mother are released from the mission and you go back to live in Salt Lake, and I want this last time to be one you will never forget," said my sister JoAnn, who had driven from Rexburg, Idaho, to Anaheim, California, with an impossible dream in her heart for me. She continued, "Remember in Shamu's act, how they have a girl come up out of the audience to get a kiss from the whale?"

"Yes," I replied.

"Well, you are going to be that girl," she exclaimed.

"You're crazy, JoAnn. There is no way I could do that. For one thing you have to be able to stand," I answered.

She calmly went on, "I have worked it all out. We will put you in your leg braces, then carry you up to the platform and lock your braces. I will stand behind and hold you while you lean out over the edge, and Shamu can come up and kiss you."

I thought for a few minutes before responding, "Well, it

might work, but the people at Sea World would never let me do it."

The next morning we put my braces in the trunk along with my wheelchair and headed for San Diego. JoAnn's friend Robyn and my companion K. K. joined in the fun.

Once inside the park, JoAnn ran over to the Shamu area and asked someone about the possibility of my being kissed by Shamu. To my surprise they answered yes. After the afternoon show would be the best time for me. A strange fear seized me—part of me did not want to do it, but part of me did, so I forced the doubts out of my mind and decided that I would try. It's a good thing I didn't tell dad or mom, for they would have fainted. Boy, this time their daughter had really "flipped her lid."

I watched Shamu's morning performance. It seemed to me that Shamu was just a little frisky that day. As he jumped out of the water, it would fly in every direction; and I could see the girl's head jerk as Shamu bumped her a little hard. *Oh, my gosh*, I thought, *I will probably fall into the tank with Shamu if he knocks me like that.* I wondered if I had enough nerve.

JoAnn, Robyn, and K. K. put my braces on me while I sat in the wheelchair, and then they stood me up to make sure I could balance well enough. The attendant from Sea World was waiting for us when the show was over, and he was anxious to help. He and Robyn carried me up the three steps to the platform, and stood me down, and then someone locked my braces. JoAnn stood behind me, holding me from the back so that I would not fall over forward. The attendant from Sea World put my right arm around his neck and supported my shoulders so I would not fall into the water.

Everything was ready. I leaned out over the water, the trainer gave Shamu the signal, and he dived under the water. It just didn't seem as if he were ever going to come up. I thought he was not in the water because I couldn't see or hear him. All of a sudden out of the corner of my eye I could see this big black shadow coming toward me. The water parted easily, and he came up so gently that I just barely felt his cool tongue against my cheek. It kind of felt like wet hamburger. Then Shamu slid back into the water and was gone. The attendant said, "I've never seen Shamu so gentle. It just seemed as if he floated out in slow motion. I have watched him many times, and this is the most gentle I have seen him."

My first trip home from the hospital is one I will never forget. Dad was not sure exactly how to get me home, so he stopped by a mortuary and asked his friend if he could borrow a slab to lay me on and carry me to the car. It was quite a distance from my room to the car, so he also borrowed a set of accordion legs to lay the slab on and push me down the hall. The accordion legs were the short legs they set caskets on. When I saw them, I almost died of mortification. I could see the use for the slab, but I could not take the accordion legs. "They are used for funerals!" I exclaimed. Dad, trying to please me, borrowed a table cart from the hospital, put me onto the slab, put the slab on top of the cart, and pushed me down the hall to the car.

I remember another night when my brother Roger came up to the hospital to take me home to spend the weekend with the family. The nurses had dressed me, helped me into my wheelchair, and put the things that I needed to take home on my lap. I was sitting a little straighter than I normally do as Roger pushed me out of the room and down the hall to the elevator. When we got to the elevator, Roger pushed the button. While we were waiting for the elevator, one of the nurses standing nearby asked me a question. I could hear her, but I was dizzy— the blood had left my head. Everything was fuzzy; though I tried to answer, nothing came out. The nurse repeated the question. Roger bent down and said, "Can't you hear? She asked you a question." Still no response. "Her hearing's gone too," Roger gasped. He must have realized I was passing out, so he tipped the chair back; as soon as the blood came back to my head, I was able to tell them what had happened. We were all laughing when the elevator came.

Each wheelchair seems to have its own personality. One Sunday I borrowed a wheelchair from the rehabilitation center so that I could attend stake conference with the family. The wheelchair had little hard rubber wheels in front, and the straps for holding the feet onto the footrest were missing, but otherwise the chair seemed to work all right.

My sister Barbara wanted to push me home because it was such a beautiful day. With help we made it down the one step and onto the straight road before us. We had not gone far when all of a sudden one of the hard rubber wheels hit a small rock. The wheelchair came to an abrupt stop, but I didn't. I went sailing out of the chair and came to rest on my stomach in the middle of the street. I rose on my elbows and turned my head just in time to see all the cars coming out of the parking lot and quickly stopping, and people running to help me. Brother Rogers reached me first, picked me up, put me back into the wheelchair, and asked, "Are you hurt?"

It was so strange not to have any sensations—I couldn't tell whether anything was hurt or broken. So I said, "I am all right." Then I turned my head to Barbara and murmured, "Let's just get out of here."

Once again we started toward home. This time both of our eyes were glued to the road watching for small rocks. The chair seemed to be moving strangely, and we couldn't tell what was the matter. So Barbara stopped to see if the brakes were on. Neither of us could believe it. Without straps to hold my feet on, both feet had slipped off the footrests and were dragging under the chair—I couldn't tell it. This was the first day I had worn my new black patent leather shoes, but we couldn't help laughing when we saw that both the toes of the shoes were worn off from dragging. "Well, you have to admit, Barbara, I fell gracefully," I laughed, as we started for home once again.

How about the day I was sitting in my wheelchair waiting for therapy. It had not been long since my accident, and my hair was starting to grow out. I finished with therapy, and as mother was taking me back to my room an elderly gentleman approached us, patted me on top of my head, and said, "Sure is a good-natured fellow, isn't he?" I guess it wouldn't have been so bad if I had not been so proud of my long, painted fingernails—I thought they looked especially feminine.

Grandpa and grandma would come to visit us periodically, but grandma couldn't understand why I couldn't walk. Really, I looked quite healthy sitting up in the chair. I would see her looking at me out of the corner of her eyes and swinging her own leg, and I knew she was thinking that I could swing mine if I tried. Pretty soon she would come over to me and say, "Becky, I think you could walk if you would just try. Now just swing your leg." She would show me how by swinging hers a little bit. I would try to explain that I could not walk, that I could not move. I was paralyzed. And she would reply, "Well, I think you can. If you would just swing your leg." Then she would show me again.

One day when we were all in the front room, I was tired of sitting in my wheelchair so dad helped me down onto the carpet. I was lying on my stomach and was practicing moving a little bit. I pushed up with my arms as far as I could go, and to my surprise I came to a kneeling position because I was wearing tennis shoes which would not let the rest of my body slide. There I was in this wobbly position. Without control of any back or stomach muscles, my stomach hung low and my back dropped in. I was a sight. Grandma looked up from her chair, saw my back, and exclaimed, "Rex, there's something wrong with that girl's back!"

The night I represented the Easter Seal Society as Miss Handicap of Utah gave Ken and me a laugh we have often talked about. Ken had to drive up from Provo and was in such a hurry that he barely made it in time to pick me up and take me to Hotel Utah. When we got here we couldn't find a close parking place, so we got out and let the attendants at Hotel Utah park the car. After a lovely evening we came out of the back door of Hotel Utah and waited with the rest of our group for our cars to be brought up. First of all, a beautiful shining

Lincoln Continental came. Next was a brand-new Cadillac. Each car looked fancy to me. All of a sudden Ken said, "Oh, no."

"What's wrong?" I asked.

"One thing I wanted to do before I came was wash my car, and I forgot to get it done. I just didn't have time," he explained. I hadn't noticed the car in all the hurry. All of a sudden from out of the tunnel came the little gray Volkswagen, covered from bumper to bumper with mud. Overcome with embarrassment, Ken pushed my chair out and said, "Get right in and don't look back." He hurried and put the chair in the car and drove out of there as fast as he could. We laughed about it all the way home.

I will not forget the night JoAnn took me to the zoo. We had our two little nieces Angela and Amy with us. We could not go to the zoo in the middle of the afternoon as it was too hot. So I called and found out that we could enter the zoo any time before six, and we could stay as long as we pleased. We got to the zoo just in time to buy tickets and get in before it closed. We had a wonderful time at the zoo. I loved looking at all the animals. When I noticed that most people were leaving, an eerie feeling came over me. I wondered how I was going to get out of the zoo, but I figured there must be some kind of gate.

I looked around and saw another lady in a wheelchair. *Oh, if she can get out, so can I,* I thought. *I won't worry any more.* We let the little children play on the swings and pet the animals in the petting zoo. I noticed the other lady in the wheelchair was getting ready to go, so I thought I would watch and see how she got out. Her husband pushed her up to the gate. (The gate was the kind which is divided in thirds by horizontal bars. You just push it as you go through and it goes around. It will only go forward, and when you get to a certain point you step out.) To my amazement this lady hopped out of the wheelchair and walked out of the gate. Her husband folded up the chair and pushed it out. That eerie feeling returned. "I don't think I can get out of the gate because I can't walk," I said to JoAnn.

JoAnn left us at the gate and went to see if there were any

workers or a zoo keeper or anyone who could unlock a gate for us. It was getting dark by then, and Angela and Amy were afraid. They thought some animals were going to get them. Angela suggested that we say a prayer; and they both knelt down on the sidewalk by me and asked Heavenly Father to help us get out of the zoo. In the meantime JoAnn, not finding anyone, climbed over the zoo wall, drove the car back up to the gate, and opened the car door on my side. Then she climbed back over the zoo wall to get to us. "JoAnn, you can't carry me out to the car," I exclaimed. I was taller than she, I weighed more, and I could do nothing to help her lift me. Besides, there was barely enough room for one person to fit in the section of the gate, let alone two of us.

"There's no other way," JoAnn replied. I held my breath as she picked me up, holding one arm around my back and the other under my knees. I had been sitting for quite a while, and my legs wanted to straighten out. Well, we started through the gate, but my feet didn't fit in the section. We couldn't push the gate backwards, so JoAnn had to put me in a standing position and carry me that way. It was a miracle we didn't get caught in the gate, but somehow we made it through. She set me on the front seat of the car, and then had to climb back over the wall to bring the children and the wheelchair out.

One afternoon during the Miss Handicap America Contest held in Denver, Colorado, the sponsors arranged for all the contestants to be taken to Colorado Springs to have lunch in a beautiful hotel. When we got there, we discovered name tags by each plate—the seating was prearranged, and mother was sitting too far away from me to be able to help. At that time I had the spoon and fork taped to my hand. I figured I could slide my fingers into the hoops by myself. Lunch consisted of a great big salad but it didn't seem as if the lettuce was all cut up, and I couldn't break it into pieces small enough to put into my mouth. In addition, the crystal water glass with its long-stemmed handle was too heavy for me to lift. I didn't know what to do. I had never been in a position like this.

The gentleman next to me asked if he could help me, but I

was too embarrassed to accept any help. I just said, "No, I'm not hungry. Thank you."

Somehow I got through the meal. For dessert the waiter brought out a plate of French pastries. At least I could pick up a pastry with my fingers and eat it. When he brought the plate to me, I was supposed to choose the one I wanted. I started to point with my index finger to the big one, but my finger didn't straighten out. And instead of pointing to the big one, it bent and pointed to one of the small ones. The waiter placed the small one on my plate. I was so surprised that I looked down. Sure enough, there was my bent finger pointing to the little one.

We stopped and I got a hamburger after we left the dinner.

Yes, happiness comes from within. It is the way we feel about life and about people. If we take the time to look around us, we can see many beautiful things made for us to enjoy that are absolutely free—a sunset, a tree, a smile, a butterfly. I love a quote that says, "The depth of our understanding is the depth of our gratitude."

As I look back and recall the experiences I have had, I can laugh now as hard as I did then. Truly, we make ourselves happy.

10

There Is Power in the Priesthood

Being raised in a priesthood home, I have come to know for myself that there is power in the priesthood. On many occasions I have been blessed by this power; and because of these blessings I have been able to accomplish the things that I was supposed to do. I remember my first experience with priesthood power. When I was five years old, our family went up Big Cottonwood Canyon to spend the night. After dad had pitched the tent, we ate dinner; and as the last flicker of the camp fire died down, we went to bed. I fell asleep, but in the middle of the night I woke up with an earache. Reaching over, I poked dad and whispered, "Dad, I've got an earache. Will you give me a blessing?" There in the darkness of the tent, dad laid his hands upon my head and through the power of the priesthood gave me a blessing; and without further pain I turned over and went to sleep.

David, his girlfriend Raelene, JoAnn and I were returning to Salt Lake after a visit with my brother Rex, who was then

president of the Northern Indian Mission, headquartered in
Rapid City, South Dakota.

We decided to return by way of Denver. We arrived in Denver
in good time and spent the first night in a motel. The next day
JoAnn and I went to West Denver to visit a family who I had
taught and seen baptized, and David and Raelene went to the
amusement park to spend the afternoon. JoAnn and I visited
and laughed with my family, the hours passing all too fast.
That night we stayed in a motel, swam in the pool, put a puzzle
together, laughed, and talked. What a great trip!

The next morning we had our prayers, stopped for breakfast,
and then headed home. We had gone as far as Steamboat
Springs, Colorado, when David noticed a high dive off to the
side of the road, and he and Raelene wanted to go swimming.
JoAnn and I decided we would stop at a shop and buy some
gifts to take home to the family. I said to JoAnn in the store,
"This scenery is so beautiful. I have never seen anything like it.
I'm not going to lie down until we get to Vernal." We bought
the gifts, and we were about ready to leave when David and
Raelene came to pick us up. As David went to put me into the
car I heard myself say, "I'm going to lie down in the back seat."
Now, I could not believe I said that, especially after I had just
made the big statement to JoAnn that I was not going to lie
down. David put me in the back seat; and they arranged a
pillow for my head, bent my knees up, and shut the door. Dave,
Raelene, and JoAnn got into the front seat and we started down
the road. We had not gone very far when out of the clear blue
sky I said, "This is the happiest time in my whole life."

All of a sudden I heard JoAnn shout, "Look out, she's
coming for us!" I felt the car swerve off the road to the left. I felt
a hard bump as we hit another car, and then I felt some rough
movement as we went down a hill and came to a quick stop in a
ditch. The impact of the stop was so sudden that it tore the
carrier off the top of the car throwing it a hundred feet over a
tall fence, and thrust the engine forward. Dave, being strong,
held onto the steering wheel column as it went through the
motor. I was lying in the back seat—my knees bent up. If I had

been sitting up, there's no telling where I would have landed, but as it was my back was protected by the seat. My knees pushed the front seat in front of me out of its tracks about six inches. JoAnn, Dave, and Raelene did not have seat belts on. It was a miracle they were not thrown through the windshield.

It was a shock to me to look out of the window and find us off the road and the car wrecked. It was not long before someone called the police. JoAnn and I went to the hospital in an ambulance. After the initial examination, the doctor decided to keep me in the hospital overnight for observation. My knee was swollen and bruised but not broken. I lay in the hospital bed all night with my leg elevated and with ice packs on it to prevent further swelling. In the morning the doctor examined me and told me that I could be released to go home in an airplane.

I had Dave call the branch and ask that two elders from the Church come and give me a blessing in the hospital. In the blessing I was promised that I would be able to make it home, but every time I tried to sit up I would feel faint and start to pass out. I told the doctor I was having this problem and asked what I could do. "That is quite common after an accident," he assured me. "Just sit up and put your feet over the edge of the bed. Do it enough times and your body will adjust." I tried, but every time I sat up I would get dizzy and have to lie down. I didn't know how I was going to get home that day as the elders had promised in the blessing.

At two o'clock when JoAnn came in to dress me, I said, "JoAnn, I can't sit up. Don't leave without me." I had to be able to sit up to go on the plane, or the airlines wouldn't take me. JoAnn dressed me, and I still couldn't sit up. David came into the room to get me. He picked me up, carried me down the corridor and out to the car, and put me in the front seat of a taxi. It was hot outside and the taxi did not have air conditioning which I needed. Because my body's temperature control does not work, if I am exposed to heat for very long I go into heat exhaustion. It was amazing. For the forty-five-minute ride to the airport I was able to sit up. When we got to the airport the air terminal was warm too, but JoAnn and Dave wet a paper towel and I kept washing off my face. The airplane landed, I was carried onto the plane, and it took off. I sat up all the way home.

Dad and other members of the family were at the airport to meet us.

What a joyous reunion we had as we hugged and kissed each other, knowing that it could have been different! One of us could have been killed in the freak accident that totaled the car. Dad carried me and put me into the car. When we got home, he carried me into the house and laid me on the bed. I tried to sit up but I couldn't. I would faint. It was a week before I could sit up without passing out. It was almost three weeks before I wanted to sit up. I knew there was power in the priesthood, and I knew that my life had been blessed. I was not only able to sit up during the long trip home, but I was also able to endure the heat.

About ten years ago during Christmastime I was riding around the kitchen in my electric wheelchair trying to decide what to buy my family for Christmas when an impression came into my mind which just said, "You are going to die." I was quite startled, and I said to myself, *Well, I have paid my tithing, I'll go to church Sunday, and I'm ready to go.* I am not afraid of dying. Sunday came and went, and I had not died. Christmas came and went, and I still had not died; yet I could not get rid of the impression that I was going to die. I remember one January night lying in bed thinking, *I don't mind if I die. I just wonder how I am going to die.* I wondered if the house would catch on fire and I would burn up because I couldn't get out or if I would fall down some stairs with my wheelchair. I just didn't know.

That night my younger brother came home from high school. He was in the kitchen, and he had a bad cough. When he coughed it seemed as if he used every muscle from his toes clear up to his neck. A shudder went through me, and I thought, *I know this is how I am going to die.* Being paralyzed I do not have use of any rib muscles and I cannot cough. It is a frightening experience not to be able to cough. I knew that was how I would die.

That week my sisters Venice and Barbara along with my grandfather, who lived with us, came down with a cough. They were very sick, and they would cough and cough. Every time I heard them cough a cold chill ran up my back. Toward the end of the week I too became sick and started to suffer with this same illness. Friday night dad and my brother Rex gave me a blessing, and dad promised me that everything would be all right. I thought to myself, *Well, everything can be all right in the spirit world too. I do not know what our Heavenly Father wants. I will wait and see what his will is for me.* Mother kept a steamer in my room, but by Sunday I could feel the cold starting to settle in my chest.

Monday night about five o'clock I was lying in my room when the door bell rang. I heard Mother go to the door. The next thing I knew Mother was at my door saying, "Becky, you'll never guess who's here to see you."

"No," I replied, "I guess I won't." As I turned and looked up, Elder Thomas S. Monson walked into my room. What an overwhelming experience to have an apostle of the Lord Jesus Christ standing in your bedroom! To this day I cannot forget it. The spirit of love and concern that he radiated touched my heart. Mother brought him a chair and he sat down and visited with my brother David, mother, and me. Dad arrived soon after and joined in the conversation.

As Elder Monson got up to leave, he said to me, "I have a blessing for you if you would like one." I had been so overwhelmed that I had not even thought of a blessing.

"Yes, I would like one," I answered. He laid his hands on my head, and with the power of the priesthood he promised me that I would get well from this affliction. He blessed the therapist and others who worked with me that they would know what to do for me. As dad walked to the front door with him to thank him for coming, Elder Monson explained, "I was coming off the freeway when an impression came to my mind to go see Becky Reeve. I thought, *Why should I go see Becky*

Reeve? It is just dinnertime and her father won't be home yet, so I kept on driving. The impression came back, so this time I turned the car around and came here." He had tears in his eyes as he continued, "I didn't come. I was sent."

This experience strengthened my testimony. I know that Heavenly Father knows us and the predicaments we are in. I know that if it is not our time to die, he will send help. The next day when the doctor came I did not have one sign of a cold. I didn't even have to sneeze. I had been healed. My grandfather and sisters suffered with this terrible cough for nearly six weeks. I know I would have died had the Lord not sent this special blessing to me.

The priesthood has blessed me many times in my life, especially since I have been paralyzed and have needed extra help on many occasions. Without this power I would not be able to do what I have done. At the time mother and dad got their mission call I was physically weak. If I overdid one day, I would be down a couple of days to recuperate. I will never forget the day dad was set apart as mission president by Elder Howard W. Hunter. After mom and dad had received their blessings, Elder Robert D. Hales suggested that if I desired a blessing from Elder Hunter, I should ask for it. I was grateful for the opportunity to have a blessing to help me fulfill this mission. Elder Hunter gave me a beautiful blessing, promising me, among other things, that my health would be stabilized. I went into the mission field not knowing what to expect as far as my health and strength were concerned.

The hours were long. The pace was fast. There were many meetings to attend each month. Yet I was able to go to every meeting and to participate in the full mission program. Many days I would sit up for eighteen hours, come home for a few hours to sleep, awake rested and ready to go again. I had never been able to do that before. I knew the Lord had blessed me.

In January, 1978, dad, mother and I were in the mission field. There had been extra pressure on us for several months. In

April dad was called to be in the First Quorum of the Seventy. Dad and mother left the mission field to attend general conference. I had been with them when dad was set apart as mission president, so I did not feel that I would go with them at this time. I was the only family member who knew of his new calling. Saturday morning when it was announced that dad had been called to serve in the First Quorum of the Seventy, the rest of the family called me. My brother Roger felt that we should all be together with mom and dad at this special time to give our support and to show our love. He left me in charge of getting the family together Sunday. Frantically I called my sister Barbara and her husband Lane in Missouri. They had gone to conference themselves and did not get home till late in the evening. They were lucky and booked a flight the next morning. My plane would arrive within ten minutes of theirs. Roger and his family left Phoenix Saturday to drive through the night so that we could all be in Salt Lake by noon on Sunday.

I was tired, excited, and exhausted from the long day of planning and working. My companion K. K. and I had a birthday party in the bedroom before going to bed. It was K. K.'s twenty-first birthday. We played the tape which her family had sent, and she opened her presents. We laughed and talked together until two o'clock when we finally settled down to go to sleep. At four o'clock she woke me up to dress me. At seven o'clock the mission assistants came to take us to the airport. I was tired, and I knew I couldn't make it on my own. I asked the assistants if they would give me a blessing before I left. Once again by the power of the holy priesthood a blessing was pronounced upon my head that I would not only have the strength to make the trip, but also that I would be able to enjoy myself and be a source of strength to my family. The plane ride, the excitement of seeing my family, of being in the temple when dad was set apart, a trip to Provo, dinner, and family home evening were all part of the busy day. It was well after midnight before I was able to go to bed. That night as I lay in my bed I thought, *I am so tired. I have never been so tired in my whole life. What a beautiful day this has been! I could not have made it without the power of the priesthood.*

It was May and we were getting things ready for the new mission president. There were thousands of things to do. Mother was extremely busy and seemed to work around the clock. For two or three days in a row she put in over twenty hours a day. One Tuesday night we were having a farewell for some of our missionaries, their families and about sixty other people who had gathered in the mission home. When mother came in and sat down in the chair next to dad, she looked pale. As the meeting proceeded, she excused herself and walked out of the meeting into another room. I wondered what was wrong. When dad had finished his message, he sent K. K. out to see what was wrong with mother. K. K. reached mother's bedside to find her sweating and weak, so K. K. ran across the street for the doctor. The doctor came, briefly examined mother, and called the emergency room at the hospital, requesting that his friend who was a skilled heart doctor meet us there. Mother was suffering from a heart attack. The doctor could not find her pulse.

Dad, his assistant, and the doctor, using the power of the holy priesthood, laid their hands on mother's head and dad gave her a blessing. Instantly her pulse returned. Mother walked to the car, got in, and went to the hospital. At the hospital the doctor who examined mother said that whatever had happened, had seemed to correct itself. After two weeks in the hospital, mother came home to spend the last month in the mission home.

When we returned to Salt Lake, the heart specialist told mother that she needed open-heart surgery. One of the arteries feeding the heart had completely closed off, causing the heart attack; and yet through the priesthood blessing some blood vessels had taken over and there was no damage done to the heart itself. The surgeon was able to do a four by-pass operation on mother, giving her a new lease on life. Within six weeks after surgery, mother accompanied dad to a mission president's seminar in Seattle. Two months later mother was ready and able to accompany dad to a new assignment as Area Supervisor for the British Isles and South Africa. Her life had been spared through the power of the priesthood.

I love this great priesthood. It is God's own power. When you keep the commandments and do the very best you can, you can draw upon this power. It is greater than any doctor and greater than any other force I know. If it is the Lord's will, miracles do happen. I have seen them in my own life. I would not want to live one day without the priesthood in my home. It is through the priesthood that our lives are blessed.

11

You Must Pay the Price

I know the truth of this scripture.

> There is a law, irrevocably decreed in heaven
> before the foundations of this world, upon
> which all blessings are predicated—
> And when we obtain any blessing from God,
> it is by obedience to that law upon which it is
> predicated. (D&C 130:20-21.)

In the physical world if we want to excel in a certain area, such as dancing, writing, surgery, or athletics there is a price to pay. The price is sacrifice, discipline, practice, and work—to become great takes time and effort.

There are spiritual laws just as there are physical laws and, as the scripture says, "When we obtain any blessing from God, it is by obedience to that law upon which it is predicated." I have come to know through my years of experience that if I want a certain quality in my life and I ask Heavenly Father to help me develop it, I must be prepared to pay the price. The following verse on prayer repeats this thought:

> We ask for strength, and God gives us difficulties which make us strong. We pray for wisdom, and God sends us problems, the solutions of which develop wisdom. We plead for courage, and God gives us dangers to overcome. We ask for favors, and God gives us opportunities. This is the answer.

As a missionary, I was saddened when I knocked on door after door, house after house, and people refused to listen to the gospel of Jesus Christ. I did not want something that I was doing or saying to stop these people from having a chance to hear the truth; so in my prayers at night I would ask Heavenly Father to bless me that when I merely had the opportunity to mention the name of Jesus Christ (before the door slammed in my face), the people might know that I knew him and would feel a difference as I repeated his sacred name.

I feel that my accident and the following seventeen years have been an answer to that prayer. Though I have prayed to know the Savior better, Heavenly Father was not going to hand that knowledge to me on a silver platter. In order to know the Savior better, I had to sacrifice and to work. I had to be patient, and I had to experience heartache and love. Only then could I begin to understand the Savior. But I have come to know the Savior better, and I have come to realize more fully what he has done for me. Without a doubt in my mind, I know that Jesus Christ is the Savior of the world. He set the example for us to follow; and the more closely we follow him, the more we will know him.

Suppose you were going to be in a play and were assigned the part of Abraham Lincoln. If you wanted to win an Academy Award for your performance, you would do all you could to realistically portray Abraham Lincoln. I imagine you would read all the books you could about him. You would want to know what people had said about him, such as his description, his walk, and anything else characteristic of him. When you stepped onto the stage that night dressed in your Abe Lincoln costume, you would know Abe Lincoln as well as you know yourself.

That is also the way we learn to know the Savior. If we really want to be like him, we must study his ideas; read what he has caused to be written; learn what he has done; love the things that he loved, the people that he loved; emulate the qualities that he had; and obey his commandments. When we are baptized and confirmed members of the Church, we take upon ourselves his name. And as we grow in the gospel, we take on the characteristics of Christ. We represent him. We belong to his Church. What a thrill it is to be able to come to know the Savior better!

Since my accident I have had opportunities to speak before many groups, to share some of my experiences and to bear my testimony. I am aware that words alone have no power. You can read words in a dictionary. All I try to do is to speak some words that will catch and hold the attention of the audience, and then the Holy Spirit can touch the hearts, fill the needs, and answer the prayers of the people who listen. Before every speaking assignment I go to, I have had to overcome physical problems. It seems to me that these problems are caused by the adversary, who wants to prevent me from sharing my testimony. I know as I take each assignment that there will be a struggle. I will have to pay the price in order for the Spirit to be there. It is not all fun and games. It takes much effort and sacrifice.

Most people will never realize how difficult it is just to get ready and to go. Many times as I have gone to speak I have been so dizzy that I have felt as if I would faint. At such times, I have taken a "sit-up" pill, as I call them, to speed up my heartbeat and constrict the blood vessels. I have sometimes had to take as many as three pills before I speak. Frequently I have not felt well, but I have still gone. I have had to have faith, to reach up to the Lord for added strength. Many times dad has given me a blessing, and after I have done all I can, the Lord has blessed me and I have been able to express the feelings of my heart. The Lord allows a special Spirit to accompany the words, and often people feel the Spirit and think that it is I. I feel humbled in such a position; but I do not want the credit, because I know where the power comes from.

During the past sixteen years I have prayed many times to our Father in Heaven that I might be strengthened and my health improved so that I might get to the point where I could stand on my feet and use my muscles. Now, I know very well that he will grant the desires of my heart, but I also know that he is not going to hand them to me without some effort on my part. That is why I have been so anxious to work, to struggle, and to achieve. I know if I stopped right now, if I did not even have the faith to put forth the effort to walk, I would never walk. It takes faith in Jesus Christ and in what he says through his priesthood leaders to put forth the necessary effort to accomplish his will. There are times when health is restored fast or things happen fast, but in my case I have had the opportunity to work to gain my health and strength back inch by inch, day by day. Through faith and prayer and works I have learned to walk by faith; and in so doing, I have more fully understood that in order to receive a blessing I must pay the price.

During sacrament meeting one particular Sunday the speaker gave us this challenge: "If you want more faith, kneel down and ask your Father in Heaven to give you more faith in the Lord Jesus Christ." That statement struck a familiar note, and I thought to myself, *If anyone needs more faith, I do. I must go home and I must ask Heavenly Father for greater faith.* That night as I went to bed I pled with my Father for greater faith in the Lord Jesus Christ, unaware of the price that I would have to pay. In the quiet of the night an impression came into my mind: "There is going to be a change in your life." And I thought, *Oh, good, it's about time I got well. I should have done this a long time ago.*

The next morning after I got out of bed, I told dad about the thoughts that had come to my mind. "I don't know whether it means anything or not," I explained, "but let me just share this thought with you, and if something happens you will know and I will know that it was an impression."

"You must be very close to the Lord," he answered and said nothing more.

The next day dad and mother met with the First Presidency and accepted a call to serve as Area Supervisor over the British Isles and South Africa. This might not seem too unusual, but to me it was a new and somewhat frightening change—this time I would not go with them. I would stay home. For over sixteen years mother and dad had been by my side, giving me strength and support, caring for my every need. They had helped me to accomplish all that I had done. Now they were going. I thought to myself, *I have given up the use of my physical body; I have given up my hopes and dreams of being a mother for this life; I have given up my sweetheart; and now I am called to give up my mother and father who have been such a great source of strength to me. What will I do?* But this time I knew the answer. I knew I could and would trust the Lord.

The first night as I lay in bed with this information floating in my mind, I woke up out of a sound sleep with fear and panic inside my heart. Realizing the source, I committed myself to the Lord. Six times during the night I awoke, and each time I would dismiss the feeling of fear and panic and then I would recommit myself to the Lord. Since that time I have not had to fight those feelings. There has been a special peace in my heart, a special quiet, and I know all is okay and as the Lord wants it.

My younger brother David, his wife, Raelene, and their six-year-old son David, Jr., moved into our home, and Raelene has been taking care of me. I have been able to accomplish many things—I have spoken to numerous different groups, I have completed a BYU home study course, I have taught my Relief Society lessons, I have visited my teachers in Relief Society, I have worked on planning a missionary reunion, I have given two bridal showers, and I have planned a Rex Reeve Round-up for my family during conference. My health has been good, and I have been blessed with added strength.

When I feel myself getting lonesome or discouraged, I simply refuse to entertain those thoughts. With full purpose of heart, I reach up to the Lord, and every time he sends a peace to comfort my soul. I don't know what is going to happen tomorrow or even where I'm going to be tomorrow; but this I do know, the Lord will raise up someone to help me when I need help. Before he left, dad said, "You will find if I go and fulfill the assignment the Lord has called me to, it will be better for you than if I were home myself because you will find that the Lord will open doors and raise up people to help you." This promise is true. Doors have been opened, friends have been raised up, and many people have sacrificed to make sure that I was well taken care of.

During the summer my sister JoAnn came home from Ricks College, where she coaches the girls' basketball and volleyball teams, to complete her nursing degree. How wonderful it was to be together and to have her help care for me!

Yes, I asked for more faith, but little did I realize then that my faith would increase only at the cost of sacrifice and trust. But as I let my mom and dad go, my faith increased and so did my knowledge that Father in Heaven would take care of me. How grateful I am that prayers are answered! How grateful I am that there is a God! Truly, there is a price to pay if we want the blessings.

12

No Man Is an Island

Because my family has played a major role in my recovery, my story would not be complete without them. I picture myself as one pencil alone that can be easily snapped in two, but if I add more pencils (one to represent each member of my family) and tie them together with a string, it is much harder to break them.

My family members are an important part of my story because they have reached out and encircled me with strong bonds of love. When I could not feed myself, they fed me; when I could not walk, they carried me; when I was down, they lifted me up. My challenges have been their challenges, and each challenge has added a dimension to my life. I have not come alone—my family has helped me.

We have always lived a "Cinderella" life. It all started on March 31, 1936, when mother attended the "ball"—a semi-monthly M-Men and Gleaner dance held in the old Twelfth and Thirteenth Ward. The dance had already started when mother arrived. She spotted some girl friends and went over to visit with them. All of a sudden a girl friend nudged mom and murmured, "There's that tall, good-looking, brown-eyed boy."

Mother turned and looked up the stairs. There stood the most handsome prince she had ever seen. He was dressed in a new gray suit and wore a smile that lit up his whole face. "He's going to ask me to dance," her friend whispered. To mother's great surprise and delight, the handsome prince passed her friend by and approached her.

"May I have this dance?" he asked.

Breathlessly mother answered, "Yes," and in a few moments they were in each other's arms, whirling around to the music of the waltz. And as in *Cinderella*, they danced every dance together, unaware of those around them or how late it was getting.

This was the beginning. To help describe dad and mother better, I will tell a little about their courtship. Dad did not have a car, so they would walk together up Capitol Hill, down Memory Grove, or around Temple Square. They would study together, reading the Book of Mormon and *The Way to Perfection*. They made plans together and set goals. They had two main goals: the first, to put the Lord and his kingdom first in their lives; and the second, to raise as large and as righteous a family as possible. These are still their goals after forty years of marriage, and nothing comes before them. Dad and mother took a courtship and marriage class from David O. McKay, and upon completion of the class they asked President McKay to marry them. On February 19, 1937, Rex Cropper Reeve and Phyllis Mae Nielsen were sealed together for time and all eternity in the Salt Lake Temple by Elder David O. McKay. This marriage created my family, and many times over the years I have loved to recall the magical night at the "ball."

Whenever I think of my father, Rex Cropper Reeve, I picture a giant oak tree—an oak tree whose great roots go down deep into the ground and whose mighty branches spread open to all who seek shelter, added strength, and love. My father is a man of faith. This is a quality which his parents, Arthur Henry Reeve and Mary Amelia Cropper, both possessed. His mother was a small woman, about five feet tall and weighing less than one hundred pounds. Yet her faith was great. Dad weighed over eleven pounds at birth and had a large head which nearly cost them both their lives. Because of the difficult birth, the doctor wanted to dismember the infant and bring him out piece by piece in order to save grandma. But grandma would not hear of it. She dismissed the doctor. Then in humble prayer she pleaded with the Lord to spare the life of her unborn child, with a promise that she would dedicate him to the Lord.

On November 23, 1914, dad was born in Hinckley, Utah. It has always seemed to me that the evil force knew the value of this great servant and tried to destroy him before he was born, but through the faith of his parents his life was spared.

Dad's motto is: "If we keep the commandments and do all we can do, the Lord will open the way for us." He has always paid his tithing and a generous fast offering and kept the commandments. Time and time again, I have seen his great faith rewarded, as we have had enough to care for our needs and some left over to help others.

I also remember the dark hours when I lay in critical condition suffering from a broken neck. Dad arrived at my bedside to be with me and strengthen me. Mother, my brother Rex, and my sister JoAnn wanted to come, and the only way down was by chartered plane. Dad waited for their plane to land, but the weather was so bad that there was not much hope for a small plane to land. The plane was over two hours late, and there was no news of its whereabouts. Thinking the plane was down with his wife, a son, and a daughter dead, and another daughter in critical condition, dad went into a small room in the hospital and talked to the Lord. With his great faith and understanding he told the Lord He could have all that he had, and then he recommitted himself to the Lord's service. Shortly afterwards, news came that mother, Rex, and JoAnn were safe. But there was no doubt in my mind of dad's love and faith in the Lord.

Dad is a wonderful husband and father. I remember he would call mother on the phone once or twice a day just to tell her he loved her. Often he would find beautiful greeting cards and send them to her with a handwritten note inside. Dad and mother truly love each other.

Even though dad was busy with his work and his responsible Church callings, he always found time to support his children in their activities. He and mother went to every football game, basketball game, or wrestling match the boys or girls were involved in. They sat through horse shows and everything they could to show their love for us. We children have wonderful memories of family home evenings, family prayers, camping trips, business trips, pine nut hunts, river trips, and other family activities. Our home was always open for our friends to come, and dad always treated them with respect and made them feel welcome.

Dad and I shared a special relationship. After I was hurt, he took me many places in my wheelchair. Dad was always so kind and considerate as he helped me. I remember the first time he took me to my media class. I was scared because it was the first time I would be left alone since my accident. Before then I had always had my family or a nurse around to help me if I needed it. I would be in my lightweight wheelchair (not my electric wheelchair), and I could not make it go very well. I could not help myself if I got sick or felt faint, and I could not get my pencil if it fell to the floor.

Dad, understanding my fears, paused for a few minutes in the car before taking me to class and took time to reassure me. "Would you like a blessing?" he asked. Then with the power of the priesthood he laid his hands upon my head and gave me a blessing. I knew everything would be all right as he left me in the classroom. It was dad with his tender heart who cried all the way home.

I have watched dad for over thirty-five years, and I have never known a greater or more dedicated priesthood leader. It doesn't matter what he is called to do, he does it to the best of his ability. His desire is to teach young men how to use the priesthood and be righteous priesthood leaders in their own homes. When dad served as a mission president, he would take time with the missionaries to help them reach their full potential. The missionaries loved and respected dad because he cared about them.

I love my father with all my heart. My great desire is to find a husband just like my dad.

Behind a pair of helping hands is a loving heart. This describes my mother, Phyllis Nielsen Reeve. Mother has always had helping hands. How well I remember waking up early one morning around two o'clock feeling terrible. I rang my brass bell for mother, and in a few moments she appeared at my bedside to see what was wrong. I told her I wasn't feeling well. With a smile and gentle hands, mother went to work to comfort me.

A bed bath, an alcohol rub and a fresh gown were all part of the loving service mother rendered to me. It took an hour of her night's rest to help me, yet a negative remark never passed her lips. I felt only love and warmth radiating from her being as she worked. Once again I was comfortable and ready for sleep. Mother tucked me carefully in, and then in a low, sweet tone asked, "Is there anything else I can do to help you, sweetheart, before I go to bed?" Warm feelings of gratitude saturated every cell in my body as I looked into her warm brown eyes and tried to express my love.

Mother always has a smile on her face and a happy heart. I remember lying critically ill in the hospital following my accident, with mother at my bedside bravely trying to strengthen me by smiling and reassuring me. One time I came to and said to mother, "Why do you keep smiling so much?" Throughout the years and despite the heartaches, mother still smiles.

Mother can outwork anybody. She was always the first one up in the morning, fixing a hot breakfast for her family and sack lunches for us to take to school. I cannot remember leaving for school with ill feelings in my heart. Mom had a unique talent for keeping a happy attitude in the home most of the time, despite all the different moods of the children.

Mom always saw to it that the dishes were done and the kitchen was clean. We all learned to make our beds. "The room is half clean if the beds are made," she explained. Mother would grind the wheat and bake fresh wholewheat bread for us to eat whenever we were hungry. I remember the feelings I had as I tried to fill mother's shoes on several occasions when she and dad went on business trips. I would get up early and try to do everything I had seen mother do; but I never got it done quite the way she did, and I was terribly tired by the time they got home. I have often wondered how mother could keep going at such a fast pace year after year.

Love is the prime motivation in her life. Dad is the head of our home, and mother is its heart. She created a home full of love and security. She loves dad with all her heart and depends on his love and direction; yet in dad's absence, she presides over the home with self-confidence and love.

I have often wondered why mother worked so hard to make our home warm and happy. I am sure that the things she suffered in her childhood helped to shape her life so that she was prepared to make our home a heaven on earth. Mother was born September 29, 1916, in Carbonville, Utah, the ninth of twelve children. Her father, Abel C. Nielsen, was killed when she was seven years old. After his death, the bank foreclosed, and the family was forced to move off the farm. Grandma worked in Price, Utah, and could come home only on weekends to be with her family. The older children tended the younger ones the best they could. A year after her father died, mother's beloved sixteen-year-old sister Venice died, which left another void in her life.

Early in mother's life she tasted poverty, hard work, heartache, death, and the scoffs and scorns of classmates making fun of her clothes. Yet she also felt the love which her mother had for her children, and all of these experiences expanded her heart and gave her a greater understanding of motherhood.

We grew up in a "fish bowl," and it took a special mother to be the wife of a priesthood leader and to teach her seven children to love the Lord and his work. Except for a three-day break once in between calls, dad has had a presiding priesthood assignment all my life. That meant mother was not only a mother, but also the wife of the bishop, stake president, Regional Representative, patriarch, mission president, and General Authority. She has had to play many roles.

Her home has always been open to those in need. She has entertained orphans as well as apostles in her home. Once when a General Authority came to eat lunch at our home between stake conferences, mother served individual turkey pot pies. I remember how good it tasted and how everyone enjoyed it.

It was not easy to raise us, as we were always supposed to be the example; often others would say, "They are the bishop's kids." Mother spent a lot of time on her knees to find out from the Lord how to help each child and how to meet the needs of her family. There is not a mother on earth who is more loved by her family than Phyllis N. Reeve.

Every sister needs an example to follow, and I have one in my older brother Rex, who is two and a half years older than I. I was always glad I was a girl—Rex was big and strong, and I would have hated to wrestle with him. When I was a sophomore in high school, Rex was a senior. He was captain of the football and basketball teams, an all-American football player, president of the seminary, and voted most friendly boy. In spite of all these honors, Rex was humble and friendly to everybody. He was always kind and considerate of me.

In Rex's sophomore year at BYU, he was picked as the outstanding football player on the team. But he was injured in a football game and in a split second his life was changed. He was told he would not play any more football for that season. What a tremendous letdown! He soon developed colitis and went from two hundred forty pounds down to one hundred sixty pounds in a couple of months. His very life hung in the balance. I ached inside as I watched him slowly gain back limited strength. I wondered what he would do the first day back at football practice. He went to help coach. When I asked him how he felt, he explained, "Well, if I can't play, maybe I can help someone else!" Those words have echoed in my mind. What a great Christlike example!

I had a powerful example to follow, and when I was hurt I knew how to handle my problem—just as Rex had. It made it so much easier for me. I treasure the letter Rex sent me while he was in Tuba City, Arizona, in the Indian seminary program. It made a real impact on my life at that time. He wrote: "This experience you are having is an experience that only the greatest soul could have and still remain faithful. A weak person would curse God and die. Becky, you are such a pillar of strength to more people than you will ever know. The things you have been through, both physical and mental, I am sure no man knows or can comprehend." I was not the person that Rex described; but if he thought I could be that person, I would try harder so as not to let the Lord or my family and friends down.

My younger sister JoAnn and I have always been "best friends." We spent many hours playing together as children. We got along fine because JoAnn was a tomboy, and she would play the dad so I always got to be the mother. It is funny that we were close—I was a homemaker who loved being home, while JoAnn was a good athlete who loved sports and the outdoors. JoAnn was a hundred percenter in all she did. She had a hundred percent attendance at school, sacrament meeting, Sunday School, and Primary. When JoAnn heard that I had been hurt, she, my brother Rex and mom flew down to be with me. JoAnn was attending BYU and this was the first time she had missed school. It was at great personal sacrifice that she came to be with me.

JoAnn has a kind and generous heart. Whenever the chips are down, you will find JoAnn there helping. She is always in the background, and often no one knows where the help is coming from. JoAnn loves to teach, and she is an outstanding coach. If a girl will humble herself and be willing to work hard, JoAnn can make a champion of her.

The first Christmas I spent in the hospital could have been

dismal, but JoAnn stayed with me and helped to make it a delightful day. She was with me when I took my first walk down the hall. She bought me the sound track to Rodgers and Hammerstein's *Cinderella* as a reward for my efforts. My first watermelon in the spring comes from JoAnn. She always has a treat for me. JoAnn, while putting me on an airplane for a weekend trip to Washington, said, "Remember, Becky, if the plane goes down, I will be there to get you. You stay alive. I will be there!" I watched out of the window at the mountain ranges below and wondered how JoAnn would ever find me, and yet I knew she would. I could not stop the tears that ran down my face when I thought of the bond of love between us. JoAnn has been with me whenever I have needed her. "Greater love hath no man than this, that [he] lay down his life for his friends" (John 15:13).

Roger Warne Reeve was born one week before I turned five years old. Roger had a sunny disposition, huge brown eyes, and a smile which lit up his whole being. With his olive skin Roger looked as if he always had a suntan. We called him Bugs Bunny because he loved carrots, and every night when he went to bed he took three or four big fresh carrots to eat before he went to sleep. It was especially fun to tease Roger, and when his permanent front teeth came in he even looked like Bugs Bunny.

The best word to describe Roger would be *work*. Roger loves to work, and he doesn't stop until the job is done. Roger could fix anything that was broken. In his shop class he made a dark wood record case for the front room. I remember how tall and handsome Roger looked in his blue and white Marine uniform with a sharpshooter medal on his chest for outstanding marksmanship. Roger is a positive, happy person who makes friends easily.

It was a special day for me when Roger came to the rehabilitation center to visit me. He carried me outside for a ride in his new convertible. We had a wonderful visit. Roger was excited about his mission call to Leeds, England, although he was recovering from an accident which had almost taken his life. It seems that he was up thirty feet on a narrow beam pouring cement. The jackhammer he was using to tap the cement had a short in it, and as he started the jackhammer (which was in the wet cement) an electric current went through him which could have killed him. A fellow worker pulled the plug, and Roger fell backwards, unconscious, on the narrow beam. His life had been spared.

Roger was anxious that I meet his girl friend before he asked her to marry him. It was important to Roger that I come to know and love this special girl. Roger has been a joy to me all of his life. He wants to build me a wheelchair house as soon as I say the word. He has already drawn up the plans. Even though we are miles apart, I can expect a weekly phone call from Roger with a positive hello to brighten up my day.

My younger sister Venice was the apple of my eye with her soft dark brown eyes and dark hair. She had a little "doll" face that I loved to kiss; she was gentle and feminine and had a warm smile; she was the sunshine in our home.

Even though Venice was a little lady, she could saddle and ride her horse like a cowboy. She has loved horses since she was old enough to talk. Every picture she drew in school had a horse on it. Venice loved to ride Western, and she entered her Appaloosa Cloud in many horse shows.

Venice is good with her hands, and she has a natural talent for knitting and crocheting. She also excels in art and sculpture. With such talent Venice was a natural as a beautician.

I was happy when Venice went to beauty school—I knew I needed some help along these lines. I was the guinea pig for Venice's first haircut (which took about two hours), but it was perfect. Since then Venice has done my hair for me. One day after she had combed a wiglet in with my hair, I attended a party. Several ladies were talking about wigs and hairpieces. One lady, so sure of herself, said, "You can tell wigs and hairpieces a million miles away. For example, that lady over there has a wig on. Now look at Becky, she is natural." I smiled inside to think that Venice could make my wiglet look so natural.

Venice is still the sunshine in my life, and evidence of her talent brightens my room. A brightly colored handmade stitchery wreath of flowers, fruit, a bird, and a butterfly is framed and hangs over my bed. To surprise me for the bicentennial year, she crocheted a red, white, and blue afghan. I sleep on pillowcases embroidered by Venice, and one of my favorite dresses was sewn by Venice. Whenever I visit her, she cooks my favorite foods, such as mild pizza smothered with black olives or carameled popcorn or homemade bread and frozen raspberry jam. Many of my treasured keepsakes are letters from Venice. If I searched the whole world over, I could not find a sweeter friend.

There are eleven years difference between my youngest sister, Barbara, and me; yet there is a love between us that goes beyond this life. Barbara was a blessing to me; she had the talent and ability to care for me after I was hurt. She was only twelve years old when I was first released from the hospital, yet she could dress me and care for my needs. I felt secure in Barbara's hands. We shared the same bedroom during her high school days, and we also shared our hopes and dreams— sometimes into the wee hours of the morning. It was during these talks that I came to fully appreciate the greatness of her soul.

Barbara also had a love for horses. She could ride and jump her horse Captain as if she were part of him. She won blue ribbons because of her talent. In fact, in anything Barbara tried, she excelled. She sewed the English riding outfit which she wore in the horse shows, she made herself a coat, and she made her wedding dress. In addition, she has made several suits for her husband and many clothes for me.

Barbara often takes me shopping; we both love to look at all the pretty things (even when we can't buy anything). Once after shopping, we discovered that someone had parked too close to my side of the car so I couldn't get in. It was snowing, we weren't wearing coats, and Barbara was obviously pregnant. What a sight! She backed the car out so that we were blocking traffic, ignoring the backed-up cars honking at us. She helped me into the front seat and then put the wheelchair in the trunk. I always wondered what people must have thought.

Barbara embroidered this saying and had it framed for me. "How beautiful a day can be when kindness touches it." My life is beautiful because Barbara has touched it. No hour is too long or too late; when I need Barbara, she is at my side.

David Arthur Reeve, my youngest brother, was well named. David means beloved, and I truly love this brother. I was thirteen years old when David was born, and I loved him as my own. He had dark brown eyes, dark hair, and a smile that filled his face. He had a tender heart and was born a peacemaker. He has a magnetic personality which draws all types of people to him. David will make a great lawyer because he can argue and win others over to his point of view. He always sticks up for the underdog who is unjustly wronged.

I was with David from the Christmas morning mother brought him home from the hospital until he made his own home. I sat through his football games, basketball games, wrestling matches, and supported him in all he tried to do. When I came home from the hospital David was there. He stood by me and helped me to make it. Even when he was only twelve years old, he could get me and my wheelchair over steps or any other obstacle. I weighed fifty pounds more than he did, but he could lift me in and out of the car. I felt secure and confident with David; I was sure he could handle any situation.

David is fun to be around. One day after washing and polishing his Corvette, he carried me out to it for a ride. The top was down, and I felt a surge of freedom as the wind hit and cooled my face. As we rode we talked about the love we shared for our family and all the blessings we had been born with. Those hours we will treasure forever.

David has always treated me like a queen. I remember the Sunday morning my plane landed in Salt Lake. After all the passengers filed out, I expected to see the men who would help me, but instead there stood David. He was dressed in a dark blue suit and had a warm welcoming smile on his face. He didn't wait for help but instead picked me up in his arms, carried me off the plane to my wheelchair, and pushed me into the air terminal to meet with the rest of the family. David's great physical strength is matched only by the size of his heart.

No man is an island. I certainly am not, for I am part of a great continent which is made up of my family members, their mates, and their children. Strengthening my shores are my wonderful friends. I wish I could write about each one and try to explain how they have blessed me. I don't suppose my earthly possessions would amount to more than a few hundred dollars; but because of my family and friends, I am the richest person in the world.

13

The Spirit
Knows No Handicap

An eagle could not soar if the wind did not offer resistance, and so it is with the spirit. In order for the spirit to reach great heights, there must be opposition. Any process which would strengthen a spirit would have to subject that spirit to conditions which would refine, purify, and test it.

What is the spirit being prepared for? The greatest of all destinies, to become like our Father in Heaven. Because our Father has such great love for his children, he laid down a plan for them to follow which would make it possible for them to return home and live with him forever. But as with anything of great worth, there is a price that must be paid and requirements that must be met, but the glorious reward far overshadows the sacrifice.

Part of God's plan was for us to come to earth and gain physical bodies in which to house our spirits. The challenge we meet here is to teach our spirits to control our physical bodies, to rise above the physical appetites of this world and become pure and holy in our thoughts and actions.

Another important part of our Father's plan was to allow us

to make our own choices and to give us experiences on earth that would try us and teach us to walk by faith. All of this was to see if we would trust our Father in Heaven and keep his commandments.

Our Father in Heaven sent his Beloved Son, Jesus Christ, to die for us so that we might all be resurrected. And more than this, Jesus Christ atoned for our sins. If we will repent and keep his commandments, we can again return and live with our Heavenly Father.

What a marvelous plan our Father has provided for us! Another exciting feature of the plan which shows God's great love for us is that he has provided us with all the necessary instruction and priesthood power. He has blessed us with parents, a living prophet, scriptures, priesthood leaders, home teachers, teachers, and opportunities for learning and growth. Heavenly Father has made it possible for each of us to communicate with him through personal prayer, and he has given us the priceless blessing of having the Holy Ghost to guide us in the path of truth. As far as I can see, the Lord has left no stone unturned in helping us find our way back to him. The rest is up to us!

I feel that once we truly understand our Father's plan, his great love, and his desire for us to return to him, the challenges we are called to face become blessings to us. As we keep the commandments, reach up to him for added strength, and overcome each challenge, our spirits grow and we begin to understand and know our Father in Heaven. I have learned to love this verse which describes these same feelings.

> I walked a mile with pleasure;
> She chatted all the way.
> But I was none the wiser
> When pleasure went away.
>
> I walked a mile with sorrow;
> Not a word said she.
> But, oh, the things I learned
> When sorrow walked with me.

On several occasions friends have expressed sympathy that I have had to suffer such a severe handicap, but I do not feel that I have suffered. It is true that I did not ask for this particular challenge in my life, but I knew from the beginning that I could trust the Lord. I realized that this life was the test, not the reward, and that if I reached up to the Lord, he would help me overcome the challenges and would bless me. It would not be easy, but with his help I could make it one step at a time. As I turned my heart, desires, and very life over to God, marvelous things began to happen.

Elder Ezra Taft Benson of the Council of the Twelve explained this principle.

> Men and women who turn their lives over to God will find out that he can make a lot more out of their lives than they can. He will deepen their joys, expand their vision, quicken their minds, strengthen their muscles, lift their spirits, multiply their blessings, increase their opportunities, comfort their souls, raise up friends and pour out peace. Whoever will lose his life to God will find he has eternal life.

Each of these promises has been evidenced in my life. I have been inconvenienced these past years, but the Lord has carried the burden. I know the Lord has blessed me. Instead of feeling bitter, I have tasted sweetness and even joy. Instead of knowing hopelessness or defeat, I have wanted to fight back and succeed.

When the body is paralyzed but the mind continues to work, the long, idle hours can be dangerously destructive. I can see how it would be easy to entertain thoughts of self-pity or hopelessness, but I have come to know that there is a door in my mind and I do not have to think about or dwell on negative thoughts. I can slam the door and replace the negative thoughts with positive, faith-filled thoughts. When I slam the door shut in my mind, I think about a few choice scriptures that I have memorized.

> But that the world may know that I love the Father; and as the Father gave me commandment, even so I do. Arise, let us go hence. (John 14:31.)

> And I was led by the Spirit, not knowing beforehand the things which I should do (1 Nephi 4:6).

> I will go and do the things which the Lord hath commanded, for I know that the Lord giveth no commandments unto the children of men, save he shall prepare a way for them that they may accomplish the thing which he commandeth them (1 Nephi 3:7).

I also think of the words to a song, such as "I Am a Child of God," "I Need Thee Every Hour," "Love One Another," or "I Walked Today Where Jesus Walked." I have memorized most of my patriarchal blessing and my father's blessing, and I go over the promises in my mind. Sometimes I bear my testimony to myself, and I reach up to the Lord and ask for strength. By the time I have finished, I always feel deep gratitude and love for my Heavenly Father and a peace that quiets my soul.

I constantly try to keep busy with a project or something I can do to lift another soul. I love to think about things I can do for others, such as making a birthday present, a special thank-you note, or a surprise for my family. I have designed and painted pillowcases; typed some of my favorite sayings or scriptures and had them copied to send to friends; and created a luncheon cloth for my mother for Mother's Day, picturing all the handprints of the grandchildren. I have found that as I voice a desire to accomplish a goal, there are many friends ready to help me. I have received great joy in planning and making gifts for friends. There are people all around who need someone to care, and the greatest joy I receive comes from helping others. Some people feel that if they could visit the sacred spots where Jesus walked, they would feel close to the Savior; but I agree with my father who said, "I do not think you can get closer to the Savior than when you bend down and lift another soul up.''

Yes, I love being alive. My life has been full and rich. I have been blessed with a wonderful family and many outstanding friends and relatives. I have had many choice experiences which have enriched my life and many challenges which have caused me to reach up to the Lord and walk by faith. I am thankful for each experience because of the things I have been able to learn through them.

But most of all I am grateful for the sacred relationship I have had with my Father in Heaven. For as long as I can remember I have had a feeling of warmth and love for him deep inside my heart. My whole desire has been to serve him and to keep his commandments. I have heard his voice through the scriptures; and from my experiences I have come to know him. I have received revelation when needed from him to guide and direct my life. I love him with all my heart, and I know that he loves me and watches over me. The words of the hymn "How Firm a Foundation" have strengthened my soul.

Fear not, I am with thee, O be not dismayed,
For I am thy God and will still give thee aid;
I'll strengthen thee, help thee, and cause thee to stand,
Upheld by my righteous, omnipotent hand.

When through the deep water I call thee to go,
The rivers of sorrow shall not thee o'erflow,
For I will be with thee, thy troubles to bless,
And sanctify to thee thy deepest distress.

When through fiery trials thy pathway shall lie,
My grace, all sufficient, shall be thy supply.
The flame shall not hurt thee; I only design
Thy dross to consume and thy gold to refine.

The soul that on Jesus hath leaned for repose,
I will not, I cannot, desert to his foes;
That soul, though all hell should endeavor to shake,
I'll never, no never, no never forsake!

I know that God lives and that he has a glorified body of flesh and bones. *I know* that he loves us and will direct our lives if we will ask. *I know* that he cannot help us return to him unless we keep his commandments.

I know that Jesus is the Christ, the Son of the Living God, and that there is no other name by which we can come back into the presence of God. *I know* that Jesus suffered for our sins, and that his atonement is effective in our lives if we will but repent and keep the commandments.

I know that the church of Jesus Christ, which has the power and authority to exalt man, was restored to the earth through the Prophet Joseph Smith. *I know* we have a living prophet of God on earth today, who guides and directs the Church through revelation from the Lord Jesus Christ.

I know this life is a test to see if we will do all things whatsoever the Lord commands. The reward comes after the test of our faith. I testify to you that as you learn from each opportunity and challenge that comes to you, you will become the kind of person you have always wanted to be; and when mortal life is over, you will be grateful for each experience because through them you will have become like God. We must be faithful to the end and keep the commandments so that we may all live forever in the presence of God.

Yes, life is a precious gift. It is filled with opportunities and challenges. It is different than we think it is going to be, and yet if the spirit is strong, life can be full and rich. The spirit comes from above. It knows no physical bounds; it is eternal; it moves in the realm of the divine. Is anything too hard for the spirit?

The physical body may be confined to a wheelchair or a bed, but the spirit can soar—the spirit knows no handicap.

Bishop and Sister Rex C. Reeve and family,
Rex Jr., JoAnn, Roger, Becky—summer 1947

Becky—fall 1958

*Western States missionaries, Sister
Ann Cox (left) and Sister Becky Reeve—
January 1962*

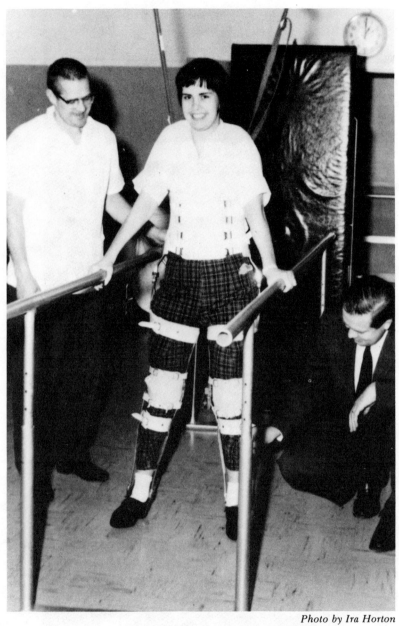

Becky in new braces—Dr. Parley W. Madsen
(kneeling) and therapist Lex Marcusen look on

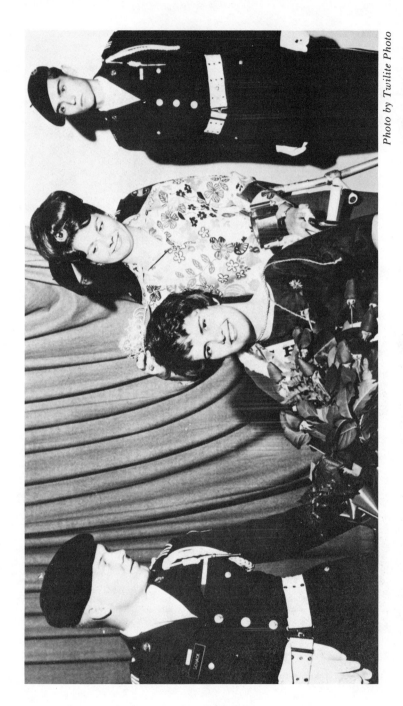

Photo by Twilite Photo

Miss Handicap America, Sharon Glasglow, crowns Becky Miss Handicap Utah 1964

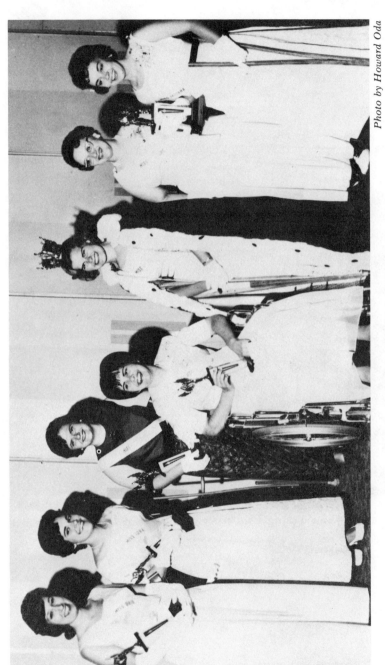

Becky is first runner-up to Miss Handicap America 1964

Photo by Howard Oda

Brigham Young University graduation—August 1974

Rex and Phyllis Reeve

Photo by Bob Fagley
The Reeve family—back (left to right), David, Roger, Rex Jr.;
front, Barbara, Venice, JoAnn, Becky

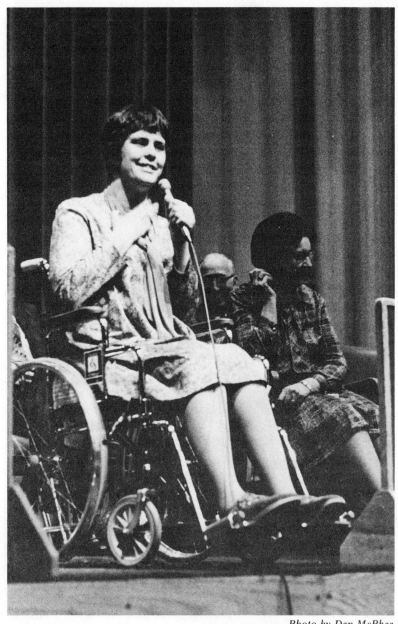

Photo by Dan McPhee

Becky speaking at Eternal Values Night
at Ricks College—March 27, 1979